LP
813 Brown BOC
Bock, Darrell L.
Breaking the da Vinci code
answers to the questions ev
SBC 1066578152
DEC '02

WITHDRAWN

WORN, SOILED, OBSOLETE

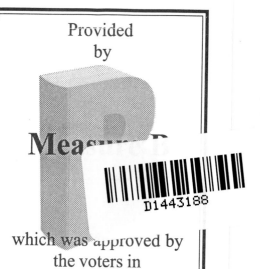

Provided
by

Measure B

which was approved by
the voters in
November, 1998

D1443188

Breaking the
DaVinci Code

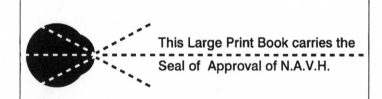
This Large Print Book carries the Seal of Approval of N.A.V.H.

Breaking the
DaVinci Code

Answers to the Questions
Everyone's Asking

Darrell L. Bock, PH.D.

Thorndike Press • Waterville, Maine

To my wife, Sally Bock, and her two sisters,
Martha Sheeder and Elizabeth Volmert,
who encouraged me to write this book
and asked many of the
good questions it answers.

National Association for Visually Handicapped
serving the partially seeing

As the Founder/CEO of NAVH, the only national health agency solely devoted to those who, although not totally blind, have an eye disease which could lead to serious visual impairment, I am pleased to recognize Thorndike Press* as one of the leading publishers in the large print field.

Founded in 1954 in San Francisco to prepare large print textbooks for partially seeing children, NAVH became the pioneer and standard setting agency in the preparation of large type.

Today, those publishers who meet our standards carry the prestigious "Seal of Approval" indicating high quality large print. We are delighted that Thorndike Press is one of the publishers whose titles meet these standards. We are also pleased to recognize the significant contribution Thorndike Press is making in this important and growing field.

Lorraine H. Marchi, L.H.D.
Founder/CEO
NAVH

* Thorndike Press encompasses the following imprints: Thorndike, Wheeler, Walker and Large Print Press.

Contents

Foreword

Millions of people who subscribe to the Judeo-Christian faith tradition believe that there is only one God, Creator of the universe (Gen. 1:1–2:24). They further believe that the women and men of what the New Testament calls "the world" turned away from their Creator. In this way sin entered the world (Gen. 3:1–11:32; Rom. 5:12). God, however, so loved the world that He sent His only Son (John 3:16). This preexistent Son of God entered the human story by taking on human flesh (John 1:14). It is interesting that the New Testament reports of this event do not open with the same emphases in telling the beginning of the story, with only John explicitly affirming Jesus' preexistence. The gospel of Mark does not suggest that Jesus was the incarnation of a preexistent Son, and Matthew (Matt. 1–2) and Luke (Luke 1–2) tell of a human birth, the result, however, of the initiative of the Spirit of God. Only the gospel of John presents Jesus' entry into the human story as the incarnation of the Word of God who existed in union with God from before all time (John 1:1–2, 14).

Across the New Testament, from Paul to Mark, Matthew, Luke, and John, and the less-well-known documents such as 1 Peter and the letter of James, a similar variety of stories tell of the way Jesus of Nazareth offered humankind the possibility of returning to a union of peace and love with God, and returning to be with that God at the end of all human history. Continuing a Jewish understanding of history, Christians believe that God made all things well at the beginning, and that the same order and beauty will be reestablished at the end of time. But the in-between-time, between the original glory narrated in the book of Genesis and the promise of the future glory noted throughout the Old and the New Testaments, also has been transformed. According to the New Testament and all subsequent Christianity, the death and resurrection of Jesus have generated a "new creation." Human beings no longer have to wait for the end of time for the restoration of God's order. Because of the death and resurrection of Jesus, a newness of life and freedom may be found in the Christian community. Experiencing baptism into

Christ Jesus and sharing in a faith community anticipate God's promises, and believers live in the joyful tension between the given of the "now" generated by the life, teaching, death, and resurrection of Jesus, and the enduring hope of God's promise of final glory.

There are, of course, many variations on this central statement of the Christian faith. In the best sense of the word *story,* this Christian story (an account of God's action that cannot hope to exhaust the *facts* but gives witness to *truth* by means of narrative) is the source of faith, love, and hope for millions of people. Yet small but extremely vocal groups of serious scholars, many of them working in important scholarly centers, some of which exist because their founding figures wished to reflect seriously upon the Christian story, have been working to demolish this account. Attempts to undermine the Christian tradition — to show that it is a fraud, with no basis in fact or reason — are not new. What is interesting about the contemporary attempts to do so is their scholarly basis. For some decades now the Jesus Seminar in the United States of America has attempted to establish a scientific method that will establish *with scholarly certitude* an account of the person, the message, and the death and resurrection of Jesus.

This is not the place to rehearse their methods, but we ought to notice where they have led the group. The Christian story, outlined above, is based upon what we call the canonical Gospels: Matthew, Mark, Luke, and John. For the Jesus Seminar, these documents have been so influenced by the theological imagination of the early Christian church that they are virtually useless. This is not new; the form critics of the early decades of the twentieth century regarded the canonical Gospels as historically unreliable. What is new for the Jesus Seminar, and those who follow them, is an attempt to replace the traditional Gospels with a speculative document known as Q and the second-century *Gospel of Thomas*.

The Gospels as we know them should be taken off the shelf, and in their place we should be devoting our attention to the speculative reconstruction of a document that was earlier than both Luke and Matthew, and was used by both of them. Members of the Jesus Seminar claim to be able to trace the history of the development of Q, its theological tendencies, and the communities that produced it. They have even published what they call a critical edition of Q.

A new meaning of *critical edition* has entered scholarship. No longer is it the establishment of an edition based upon a critical reading of all extant editions, but a comparative study of what *scholars* say about a document that we do not have. The *Gospel of Thomas*, reflecting Gnostic tendencies of second-century Christianity, is nevertheless regarded as carrying more authentic historical traditions than Matthew, Mark, Luke, and John, all of which were written between 70 and 100 C.E. based upon traditions that are earlier than them. The action of God, in and through Jesus Christ, as told in the tradition of Gospels, should be bracketed out of the discussion for the moment, while we rediscover what Jesus *really* said and did, and what *really* happened at His death.

A further important scholarly activity has emerged from the discoveries of a Gnostic library in Upper Egypt at a place called Nag Hammadi. Prior to this discovery, our knowledge of Gnosticism, a form of Christianity that blossomed in many forms from the second to the fourth century, came to us from mainstream Christian fathers of the church. These Fathers' works refuted them, while citing them at great length in their refutation. Now we have firsthand Gnostic documents (although they are generally

Coptic translations of original Greek texts). These texts show that there were a variety of interpretations of the Christ story and a variety of ways in which Christian life was lived. This important and helpful discovery deserves scholarly attention and respect. However — and this issue is discussed at further depth in the rest of the book — many fine scholars are suggesting that the Christian story, loved by millions and described above, has been imposed upon the Christian church by imperial and ecclesiastical authority. In other words, for almost two thousand years, Christians have been subjected to the mushroom treatment. If you want mushrooms to grow, you keep them in the dark and feed them rubbish. A return to a more authentic historical basis (the Jesus Seminar) and a recognition that Christianity in the early centuries had a number of faces that would not be recognized in the contemporary church (Gnostic studies) will produce a better understanding of what the Christian church can and should be. What millions believe is the result of their having been fed rubbish!

Flying on the coattails of these scholarly activities comes Dan Brown's *The Da Vinci Code*. I loved it! It was a great page-turner, and I read it from front to back in a flight from Newark Airport to San Francisco. But between the lines, I was able to read the background of the scholarly discussions that I have outlined here. Into that mix Brown introduces further speculation, available some years ago in a book called *Holy Blood, Holy Grail*. That earlier work described a secret guild that had its origins in the crusades. That guild possessed secret information about Mary Magdalene and her relationship with Jesus. A more recently established Catholic body, Opus Dei, adds passion, violence, secrecy, and corruption to the mix. Guilds did arise in the medieval period, and they still exist. Opus Dei is indeed a body of highly conservative people in the Catholic church, strongly supported by Pope John Paul II. Brown has knitted together these *disparate* elements — serious research, speculation about the activities of secret guilds, and the Opus Dei — into a very good thriller. What is amazing is that the book has caught the imagination of many readers. These readers are wondering whether the Christian story, as I outlined it, is purely the result of an exercise of power on the part of the Roman emperor, and the powerful suppression of alternative voices by the increasingly powerful Roman Catholic Church. When a book generates the feature article and the front cover of *Newsweek* (December 2003), it is affecting the popular imagination and calls for attention.

Such claims have little or no basis in truth. I am aware that this is not the popular thing to say, but one must be honest. It is therefore a delight to be able to introduce this fine study from Darrell Bock. The issues raised in this Foreword receive a full and respectful treatment in the book that follows. Professor Bock and I met only recently. He is a distinguished Protestant professor of New Testament. I am the dean of theology and religious studies, also a professor of New Testament, at one of America's major Catholic universities. Scholars of second-century Gnosticism have *rightly* insisted on the need to recognize that many expressions of Christianity have existed and have given life to generations of believers. I would argue that we need to accept that no single theological or ecclesial "system" can exhaust the richness of the Christian story. My brief indications of the different presentations of Jesus' entry into the human story in Mark, Matthew, and Luke, and then John are but one indication among many that there is a degree of *difference* in the proclamation of the Christian message from its birth. From my Roman Catholic tradition, I am happy to join Darrell and his Protestant tradition to affirm that the "myth" of *The Da Vinci Code* does not have a leg to stand on in its attempt to dethrone the two-thousand-year-old Christian story of what God has done for us in and through Jesus Christ. He has "broken" *The Da Vinci Code*. I trust that many will sense the openness, yet honesty, of the following pages.

Francis J. Moloney, S.D.B., D. Phil.
*Dean, School of Theology
    and Religious Studies
and Katherine Drexel, Professor
The Catholic University of America
Washington, DC 20064*

Introduction

Like millions of avid readers, I love a good read. Add a cup of intrigue, some famous historical figures, controversial institutions, exotic sites, and something to figure out, and you've got me. Entertaining fiction awakens the imagination and takes us into worlds unlike the ones we live in. Often fiction draws us in by working with realities just familiar enough to us that we are caught up in a fresh experience. That is why a good story has entertained us since Homer began to describe epic sea voyages in the *Odyssey*, hundreds of years before Jesus.

But fiction is like virtual reality, a new phenomenon that stretches the imagination. Through technology we design a world, often as we wished it might be rather than the way it is. What emerges is also intriguing and entertaining, but it is still something short of full reality. Sometimes virtual reality and reality can be very similar and hard to distinguish. Knowing the difference between fiction and reality is important, especially when it comes to claims related to God, gender, and the history of faith. This book seeks to examine such claims.

As I write, the very entertaining novel *The Da Vinci Code* sits at No. 1 on the *New York Times* Best-Seller List, where it has occupied a high perch for thirty-five weeks. The first page of the novel lets us know we are in for a different ride. We hear of a secret society called the Priory of Sion whose members include figures such as Sir Isaac Newton, the painter Botticelli (one of my favorites), Victor Hugo, and Leonardo da Vinci. Next to this group stands the Opus Dei, a Catholic organization that allegedly brainwashes and engages in coercion. The intellects of the West are lined up against faith even before the action begins. All of this is placed under the banner of "Fact." The page's final sentence hammers the point: "All descriptions of artwork, architecture, documents, and secret rituals in this novel are accurate." This remark surfaces as a kind of pop-up ad at the start just to grab our attention. But it also tells us that the story we are about to hear is set in a nonfictitious, historically accurate world. That sounds like something close to virtual reality to me.

20

So the question is raised, How accurate is this work and its claims? Was Jesus married to Mary Magdalene? Did He have children? Did the Catholic church suppress the fact that His "family" fled to France as a way to protect His claims to divinity? Did the Bible emerge as a power play document in the early fourth century under the emperor Constantine after Christianity finally won its battle with paganism? Was the role of women suppressed in the early centuries of the Christian faith? In short, did the church lie?

On the ABC News Special *Jesus, Mary, and Da Vinci*, which aired on November 3, 2003, the book's author, Dan Brown, proclaimed himself a believer in these things. In an interview on *Good Morning America* the day of the special, he declared that if he had been asked to write a piece of nonfiction on these things, he would change nothing about what he claimed in the novel. In his book, key characters state that Jesus was married and had children. Moreover, the Catholic church lied about this and suppressed the fact that His wife and children fled to France. In that interview, Brown affirmed the views of some of his novel's characters. He told the primetime audience of around 15 million viewers that after having

21

begun his quest as a skeptic, he became a believer. In fact, this is what he said: "I began as a skeptic. As I started researching the Da Vinci Code, I really thought I would disprove a lot of this theory about Mary Magdalene and Holy Blood and all of that. I became a believer."

Almost sounding like an evangelist's invitation, his confession asks us to ponder whether these things are so and why it might matter. No longer is *The Da Vinci Code* a mere piece of fiction. It is a novel clothed in claims of historical truth, critical of institutions and beliefs held by millions of people around the world.

In the pages ahead, I will examine the various claims of *The Da Vinci Code*. As a research professor of New Testament studies, I am a student of the early centuries of Christianity with specialization in what we call Jesus studies. I am a Protestant, but what I say here is not a matter of being Protestant or Catholic; it is a matter of dealing appropriately with historical data. It is my view that novelists do not necessarily make good historians, and that matters when a topic like this one is portrayed in such an entertaining way as quasi nonfiction. It is especially important when several ideas build into a huge theory — and each

22

part of the construct is suspect. It is also important when, here and there, one can spot an agenda expressed through the novel's key characters.

It would not be right just to complain, however. Our role is to explore the labyrinth of these ancient ideas and studies. Claims are easy to make on each side of a discussion. We need to consider what we know and what is debated.

This popular work suggests that these ideas are new, freshly surfacing historical data. For example, Teabing, one of the book's major characters, appeals to real, newly discovered documents disclosing new truths about Jesus, Mary Magdalene, and the earliest history of the church. In fact, much of what is woven into the novel was said in 1982 in *Holy Blood, Holy Grail*, whose back cover asks questions like these: Is it possible that Christ did not die on the cross? Is it possible that Jesus was married, a father, and that His bloodline still exists? Is it possible that parchments found in the south of France a century ago reveal one of the best-kept secrets in Christendom? Is it possible that these parchments contain the very heart of the mystery of the Holy Grail? Sound familiar? Anyone reading *The Da Vinci Code* will recognize these themes. The

23

novel alludes to the earlier work on page 253, noting it is an "acclaimed international bestseller." *Holy Blood, Holy Grail* has a blurb from the *Los Angeles Times Book Review* that reads "enough to seriously challenge many traditional Christian beliefs, if not alter them." So questions like those in *Holy Blood, Holy Grail* represent a set of ideas worth examining in more depth.

Why a Historical Investigation About a Book of Fiction?

I know that many who have read *The Da Vinci Code* have questions. Some, along the lines of the book reviewer of *Holy Blood, Holy Grail*, ask whether we should redesign our understanding of Christianity. I hope to answer many of these questions, not with the garb of fiction but with a look at the central ancient texts, some of which form the basis of *The Da Vinci Code*. With other questions, where data are thin, I hope to show where the likelihood lies.

I have had many ask why a novel should get such careful historical attention. I am told, "After all, it is only a piece of fiction!" The point might be made this way, "The author is merely having some fun with us, spinning out a mystery about topics that fas-

24

cinate us. Lighten up; it is no big deal. It is just a book." However, this is not merely any piece of fiction. The scope of what it claims as fact, the impression it leaves making those claims under the "cover" of fiction, and the fact that it addresses a significant subject for our culture's own self understanding make it important that its claims be assessed and/or appreciated. This is especially true when the area it addresses is largely unknown territory for readers of the novel. One needs a guide for the terrain. For the issues of faith and relationship to God are too important to be left to the confusing category of "historical" fiction where the claim is that despite being a novel the history is fact.

As one who specializes in New Testament studies, I have been asked repeatedly about various elements in this novel since its release. My first encounter with the issues raised by the novel came in the summer of 2003 when a reporter for Beliefnet.com asked me if I could discuss with her the question of whether Jesus had been married and the significance of Mary Magdalene to the church. She was writing a piece evaluating and discussing the theories tied to Mary. I did the interview and spent an hour or so with her on the phone diving into var-

25

ious aspects of the issues. At the time, I thought she was asking an odd set of questions, but we never know what will show up as a point of discussion in the public square.

But the same questions never went away. Next came a set of queries from a friend working in New Testament at another school as I was preparing to participate in a seminar series on Jesus that he was sponsoring at his church. He asked me to be prepared to answer questions about Jesus and *The Da Vinci Code*. I e-mailed him that I did not know much about the novel, just some of the things it was claiming. Within a week of that e-mail exchange came the invitation from ABC News to discuss the biblical basis for the novel's views, as well as a subsequent invitation to write a counterpoint, commentary piece for the network news Web site.

It was time to read the book in order to put my remarks in its context and not just in the context of what I knew about the Bible. During that reading, I decided there was something more that people needed to be made aware of and appreciate about the roots of the novel. I did the ABC interview, wrote the counterpoint piece, and agreed to do a few Sunday school classes on the book to help people sort out the claims. At the same time friends, colleagues, and even rel-

26

atives started to ask me about the issues in the book. Some of those questions reflected a sense that maybe the novel was saying something true and maybe we needed to take a fresh look at the faith. After all, could four million readers be wrong?

The last piece of the puzzle was a call from a publisher to write a book on the topic. Members of the editorial staff had seen the special and wanted to publish a work that delved into the details. I told them that the details would involve examining a series of obscure but fascinating ancient texts from various points of view. These texts would come from an array of ancient communities and authors, some Jewish and others Christian. Another group would hold to a combination of beliefs associated with both Christianity and Gnosticism, another major philosophical view of the second century. It is a world of not so familiar names like Josephus, the first-century Jewish historian; the Qumran community, a Jewish community where the Dead Sea Scrolls were discovered; and Nag Hammadi, another community where many of the so-called secret gospels now drawing public attention were found. It also would mean taking a journey through a labyrinth of issues.

I thought it could be quite a journey into a world that most people know little about but one in which I have lived for years. Like Sherlock Holmes or Indiana Jones getting to lead a tour through a mound of clues, I could help these fellow travelers read these texts and examine these ideas. I could discuss what we know about these texts, where they came from, and whether their ideas were as new as some suggest. I decided to sign on for an investigative look at these ideas, new to the general public but long discussed among historians of this period. I invite you along for the ride.

The best way through the labyrinth is to work one "code" at a time. The novel presents seven codes, issues that can be formed as questions, that are expressed or implied within its story. Our research for uncovering the validity of these codes will focus on the 325 years immediately following the birth of Christ, for the claims of the novel rise or fall on the basis of things emerging from this period.

This book is my effort to clarify the difference between virtual reality and historical likelihood. In other words, I hope clearly to distinguish the difference between fictitious entertainment and historical elements of the Christian faith. By seeing these differences, one can break the Da Vinci Code. But I warn you there are some interesting — and even alarming — surprises along the way.

As I looked closer at *The Da Vinci Code*, I began to see another code lurking behind its pages, one I recognized from my study of the New Testament and the history of the earliest church. Most readers of the novel have no idea that this other code is there. I know when I started my work on the novel, I did not see it at first. Breaking the Da Vinci Code led me to discover the presence of this other code. That is another reason I have written this book — to bring to the surface the code underneath and behind *The Da Vinci Code*. This second code will emerge as we examine the novel. Keep your eyes open for it as it emerges from the clues we will encounter. It is a key element behind why this novel has become something of a public phenomenon and why the issues it raises are worthy of careful study and reflection.

Because our study has multiple layers, we will have to consider Mary Magdalene at two distinct points of our investigation, one early and the other later. The early point will focus on her specific relationship to Jesus. Later we will return to her and try to understand why the figure of Mary Magdalene is important. But before we can do that, we must examine various ancient documents in which she appears. Some documents the church has used for centuries, and others are receiving renewed attention today in a host of studies on secret writings outside the Bible.

Like a good investigator, I now assemble the pieces of the mystery surrounding the Da Vinci Code. Each chapter will probe what we know, how we know it, and what we have to think about together. We will review several ancient texts, for they unlock much of the history that *The Da Vinci Code* attempts to portray. If you get lost, turn to the Glossary in the back that gives the history of these ancient texts, defines major terms, and summarizes the major players. Treat the Glossary like tour guide information; it is there to make sure you know where you are. If you like Sherlock Holmes or Indiana Jones, I think you are in for an adventure. Only in this case, we are dealing with both fiction and history. What is the difference between virtual reality and historical reality when it comes to Jesus, Mary, and *The Da Vinci Code*? Let's see if we can find out.

Code 1

WHO WAS MARY MAGDALENE?

We start with the key woman in our study, Mary of Magdala. In *The Da Vinci Code*, she is the wife of Jesus and the mother of His children, and that is a secret the church wanted to cover up to protect the divinity of Jesus. In the novel, she also is directly associated with the Holy Grail. The association with the Grail comes through the idea of Holy Blood and its bloodline (p. 250), the *Sangreal*. A word play on the term *Sang Real* gets us to a connection to the Holy Grail. The hypothesis is that the story of the Holy Grail really points to the holy bloodline of Jesus and Mary Magdalene coming into France. This idea is expressed explicitly in *Holy Blood, Holy Grail* as a hypothesis (pp. 313–15). In fact, the direct connection of Mary to the Holy Grail is a late, fresh twentieth-century addition to the legend of the Holy Grail. In addition, the word play it is based upon comes from the medieval period and is not a part of the original meaning of the term.

In *The Da Vinci Code*, Mary is said to be in

Leonardo da Vinci's painting *The Last Supper*. The evidence is the V shape to the left side of Jesus as one looks at the painting (p. 244). It is the symbol of the feminine, and a feminine-looking figure on the left side of the V is Mary of Magdala (p. 238 of the novel discusses this V; see the painting on our cover). Leonardo knew of the genealogical secret and put a clue of it in this painting. It is from this detail that the novel gets its title, *The Da Vinci Code*. All of these ideas surface in the middle portion of the book (pp. 242–45). So Mary is a logical person with whom to begin our study. Who was she? What was her relationship to Jesus?

Mary Magdalene has always possessed a certain mystique. In the 1960s she was often a key figure in musicals about Jesus. Interest in her has not waned and reflects a curiosity that has belonged to her almost from the beginning. Part of the reason for such interest is that there are actually so little data about her. One element of a story like Mary's is that when there is very little information, there is a desire to round out the picture. Proving or disproving what is speculated about her is hard to do. We will proceed one step at a time. We consider now only Mary Magdalene's familial relationship to Jesus, the key element in the novel's claims. In a later chapter we will return to Mary and explore the symbol that Mary has become for our culture.

Mary in the New Testament

Mary is one of seven people with this name in the New Testament, and most of them are distinguished by additional descriptions: (1) Mary, the mother of Jesus (Luke 1:30–31); (2) Mary of Bethany (John 11:1); (3) Mary, the mother of James who was not the Lord's brother (Matt. 27:56); (4) Mary, the wife of Clopas (John 19:25); (5) Mary, the mother of John Mark (Acts 12:12); (6) one otherwise unidentified Mary (Rom. 16:6); and (7) Mary Magdalene, distinguished by a reference to her home, Magdala (Luke 8:2). These descriptions help us to sort out the individuals on the list. There is no hesitation to mention one's familial status as a way of doing this. Often a connection to a male is the distinguishing feature, as with Jesus' mother, the mother of James, John Mark's mother, and especially the wife of Clopas. Such a connection reflected the patriarchal first-century culture; that is, it was culturally centered on the male. This frequent naming of females with a male connection will be a significant

33

point when we consider whether Jesus was married.

The name Mary is actually a modern form of the Jewish name Miriam. It was an extremely popular ancient name for women, which may add to the confusion among individuals. Mary Magdalene was not connected to any male, though she could have been if there had been such a connection to highlight. Rather, Magdala, where she lived, identified her. So Mary Magdalene was Mary from Magdala. Magdala is probably modern-day Migdal, located near the Sea of Galilee in Israel. Jesus' main ministry took place in the Sea of Galilee area.

Mary Magdalene in the New Testament

The biblical passages that discuss Mary from Magdala come in four groups.

First, she was a disciple who was the beneficiary of an exorcism by Jesus and was part of an entourage of women who supported and traveled with Jesus and His disciples (Luke 8:1–3). Having several women travelers was not as unusual as having Mary Magdalene travel with the group of disciples on her own would have been.

Second, she was present at the cross, a

witness who no doubt was sad about Jesus' fate (Matt. 27:55–56 with the mother of James and Joseph and the mother of the sons of Zebedee; Mark 15:40–41; John 19:25). In each note about her presence at the cross she was not alone, but was part of a larger group of women. Matthew described the women as those who had followed Jesus from Galilee, ministering to Him. Mark identified the women as people who followed Jesus in Galilee and ministered to Him. John's description was similar. Mary was not singled out, but was part of a group of women, and many of the women at the cross were connected to known males. Had there been such a connection between Mary and Jesus, there was plenty of opportunity to make the point about Mary Magdalene in these earliest texts.

Third, some texts placed her at the cross either as or after Jesus was laid to rest (Matt. 27:61 with the "other" Mary; Mark 15:40 with Mary, the mother of James the younger and of Joses, and Salome, along with many other women). In other words, the named women were prominent among the women noted. Once again, Mary was not singled out on her own.

Fourth, all of the remaining biblical texts about Mary Magdalene depict her as a witness to Jesus' resurrection. According to Matthew 28:1, she returned with the "other" Mary to anoint the body, which they still expected to be there on the third day after the Crucifixion. Mark 16:1 is similar to the list involving Mary, the mother of James, and Salome. In English translations that refer to Mark 16:9, she is mentioned as one to whom Jesus appeared and as a beneficiary of an exorcism, combining what the Resurrection accounts and Luke 8 tell us elsewhere. (There is scholarly discussion about whether Mark 16:9–20 was an original part of Mark, but that issue need not detain us; nothing here is added to what the undisputed texts tell us.) Luke 24:10 names Mary as a member of the entourage — Joanna (noted in Luke 8:2–3) and the mother of James and an unspecified number of "other" women — that announced Jesus' resurrection to the apostles and others. No one believed their report at the time. The biblical accounts are amazingly honest in admitting that the disciples did not anticipate Jesus' resurrection.

By far the most dramatic account is Jesus' appearance to Mary in John 20:11–18; this is the only place in the New Testament where Jesus and Mary Magdalene were alone together. She was clinging to Him so that Jesus told her to let go. Such behavior was unusual in the Jewish culture and would be frowned upon in normal circumstances because public displays of affection between nonrelated persons generally were not culturally affirmed, except in the case of a greeting like a holy kiss (Rom. 16:16). The emotion of the moment caused Mary to grab Jesus out of surprise and joy. There was nothing sexual about what happened, as some have suggested. She simply reacted spontaneously, welcoming His surprising, new existence with an embrace. The reaction is understandable when one appreciates that she thought Jesus was dead and gone and that she had already said her last good-byes to the teacher who had turned her life around.

She left the scene, a witness to Jesus' resurrection (John 20:18). She carried out the announcement of resurrection that the risen Jesus told her to proclaim. She was an *apostle*, not in the technical sense of the Twelve whom Jesus appointed to lead the disciples but in its more common usage as a "sent, commissioned messenger." We shall return to this apostolic role in a later chapter. It is the most important point about Mary that the Gospels tell us.

This is the entire inventory of New Testa-

37

ment references about Mary Magdalene: eleven passages total (twelve counting Mark 16:9). She was a disciple and traveling supporter of Jesus among a group of other women. She was never related to Him in any other sense. Although other women in the group were connected to males as relatives, Mary was not. She was a witness to the Cross, the burial, and the Resurrection. That was it.

Mary Magdalene in Key Texts Outside the Bible

The Church Fathers

Early church references to Mary Magdalene, except in Gnostic and related materials, which we shall consider separately later, fall into this same pattern. She was a faithful disciple, a follower of Jesus who witnessed Jesus' death, burial, and resurrection.

There is an interesting text by Hippolytus, a third-century church father. (A church father refers to a major church leader during the earliest centuries of the church.) The case begins by noting that there is a reference among early Christians to Mary as an "apostle to the apostles" (Ann Graham Brock, *Mary Magdalene, The First*

Apostle, p. 1). Some also claim the term refers to the acceptance of Mary's high rank in the church (Brock, p. 161, n. 2), but a closer look at this text shows it does not make a point of rank, nor does the title in the singular appear here. In fact, the singular expression appears to surface in an unclear way in the later Middle Ages around the tenth century. The point about rank is a deduction from the fact that Mary was among the first to see Jesus. The comment by Hippolytus appears in his commentary on the Old Testament book of the Song of Songs 24–26 (also known as the Song of Solomon). It reads, "Lest the female apostles doubt the angels, Christ himself came to them so that the women would be apostles of Christ and by their obedience rectify the sin of ancient Eve . . . Christ showed himself to the (male) apostles and said to them: . . . 'It is I who appeared to these women and I who wanted to send them to you as apostles.' "

This alludes to the commissioned witness role of *all* the women who experienced the empty tomb, although the Hippolytus passage has Mary and Martha especially in mind. This text, appearing in a passage expounding Song of Solomon, gives us another detail. The women who witnessed the

39

risen Jesus are associated with the idea that the church as a whole is the bride of Christ (Eph. 5:22–33). (The Song of Solomon was often read in the early church as being about the spiritual wedding of Jesus Christ to His church.) These women represent the church as a whole, but they do so as a group in the remarks of Hippolytus. So Hippolytus told us only that women like Mary Magdalene functioned as approved witnesses of Jesus' resurrection. We shall return in Code 6 to this text.

In the other materials from the Fathers, there is nothing particularly outstanding about Mary. Such texts describe her in terms that parallel what the biblical Gospels tell us.

A Key Gnostic Text on Jesus and Mary Kissing

Another class of texts comes from Gnostic Christian sources that emphasize the direct teaching of mysteries. We will discuss the Gnostics in more detail in Codes 4 and 5, but a famous passage involves a text that has Jesus kissing Mary (*Gospel of Philip* 63:32–64:10). This text was composed in the second half of the third century, a full two hundred years after the time of Jesus. This text describes Mary as a "companion"

40

of Jesus. Of all the passages that could suggest Jesus was married, this is the best potential case.

However, the key part of the text is broken at 63:33–36 and reads, "And the companion of the [. . .] Mary Magdalene. [. . . loved] her more than [all] the disciples [and used to] kiss her [often] on her [. . .]." The brackets indicate broken locations in the manuscript where there is no reading because the manuscript is damaged. Talk about a mystery to solve!

Working with broken ancient texts takes skill. Sometimes there is genuine debate about what the full original text said. In some cases where words are supplied in the brackets, we can logically suggest the reading because of the context and the size of the break. Specialists surmise what specific word goes in the blank by the number of letters missing and then translate the result. For example in the sentence, "My wife sent me to the stor[. . .] get some eggs," one could reasonably suggest the full sentence was, "My wife sent me to the store to get some eggs." In cases where good multiple options exist, one cannot be sure what the complete text said.

In this text involving Mary, some contend that it could affirm that she was kissed on

41

her cheek or forehead since either term fits in the break. Others prefer the reading of a kiss on the mouth because of a parallel in the *Gospel of Philip* 58:34–59:4, which reads, "For it is by a kiss that the perfect conceive and give birth. For this reason we all kiss one another. We receive conception from the grace which is in one another." This reading of *Philip* 63:33–36 is discussed in Harvard Professor Karen King's *The Gospel of Mary of Magdala*, where she prefers the option of a kiss on the mouth because of the parallel to *Philip* 58–59 (p. 204, n. 50). Her discussion also develops that although there is an explicit reference to a kiss on the mouth in *Philip* 63, the reference from *Philip* 58–59 is to the kiss of fellowship between believers, where nothing sexual is intended. It refers to "the intimate reception of spiritual teaching" (p. 146). We would note that the locale of the kiss ultimately referred to in *Philip* 58–59 is not clear.

King does not put the two observations about these two passages together, but I will. If the kiss of *Philip* 63 is similar to the kiss of *Philip* 58–59, then the reference likely is to a kiss of fellowship. If so, the kiss may be one for the cheek and not the mouth. King does suggest (correctly in my view) that the imagery is about Mary being associated with Wisdom and that this *spiritual* connection stands behind the reference (p. 145). She probably does this because these kinds of texts often carry a symbolic or spiritual sense over a more literal one, as scholars often note. Even if the reference is to a kiss on the mouth, the basis for the text pointing to something primarily sexual does not exist. The reference merely pictures a tender, spiritual relationship.

The other key term in *Philip* 63:34 is a Greek loan word found in this Coptic language text. (A loan word is simply a word borrowed from another language.) So the key term here is a Greek term. It transliterates as *koinonos* and is translated "companion." The term can mean "wife" or simply "sister" in a spiritual sense. But this term is not the typical or common term for "wife," which in Greek would be some form of *gynē*.

King asks a series of questions about this *Philip* 63 text: "Is Mary Magdalene identified with Wisdom here? Is that why the Savior loved her more than the other disciples? Does kissing mean that Mary and the Savior had a sexual relationship or was it a spiritual one?" (p. 145). King suggests that

43

Mary is seen as Wisdom in the text, making her mother of the angels, spiritual sister to the Savior, and His female counterpart. Nothing about this points to a real marriage.

The passage is full of spiritual imagery to let us know this is what the passage is saying. The reference in the passage is more likely to a spiritual relationship, given the variety of relationships that Mary has in this gospel. When one considers how frequently these kinds of texts use spiritual imagery by comparing the birth of wisdom to natural birth, the image of male-female counterparts is a part of the metaphor rather than a historical point.

So uncertainty applies to the text from *Philip* 63. We do not know the exact relationship or to whom Mary Magdalene was being related at the start of this passage, although it is likely she is said to be Jesus' companion. We also do not know where she was kissed, although it might have been on the mouth. If a kiss on the mouth is described, something unusual is indicated. The kiss does point to a level of intimacy between Jesus and Mary, but it probably represents a spiritual closeness as spiritual counterparts in the birth of creation that is associated with wisdom. It is far less likely

44

that something sexual is in view or that their marital status is being addressed.

A Text on Jesus' Favoritism Toward Mary

A final relevant passage comes from the second-century *Gospel of Mary Magdala* (hereafter *Gospel of Mary*). In it Peter was challenging the role of Mary as the recipient of a special revelation from Jesus. A controversial element of Gnosticism (or a similar Christian movement) involved the way its adherents claimed to receive additional special revelation. This text seems to reflect that conflict with Mary being portrayed in a sympathetic way while being challenged by some of the key apostles. The text is *Gospel of Mary* 17:10–18:21. It reads,

But Andrew answered and said to the brethren, "Say what you (wish to) say about what she has said. I at least do not believe that the Savior said this. For certainly these teachings are strange ideas." Peter answered and spoke concerning these same things. He questioned them about the Savior: "Did He really speak with a woman without our knowledge and not openly? Are we to turn about and all listen to her? Did He prefer her to

45

us?" Then Mary wept and said to Peter, "My brother Peter, what do you think? Do you think that I have thought this up myself in my heart, or that I am lying about the Savior?" Levi answered and said to Peter, "Peter, you have always been hot tempered. Now I see you contending against the woman like the adversaries. But if the Savior made her worthy, who are you indeed to reject her? Surely the Savior knows her very well. That is why He loved her more than us. Rather let us be ashamed and put on the perfect Man, and separate as He commanded us and preach the gospel, not laying down any other rule or other law beyond what the Savior said."

Peter was disturbed because Mary, a woman, received revelation from Jesus that the other apostles did not receive. Mary was troubled and hurt by Peter's challenge, but Levi (probably to be equated with Matthew) came to her defense: the Lord chose her for the role; Jesus made her worthy and knew her well. The implication is that Jesus knew her well enough to know whether she was worthy to receive independent revelation. Out of that knowledge came Jesus' exceptional love for her. There was no appeal to Mary's having any familial status. She was simply the beneficiary of a special revelation from Jesus. Nothing in the text indicates anything more than that Jesus appeared to her alone.

One more summary thought remains. It comes from a review by Craig Blomberg in *The Denver Journal.* He notes the emphasis on Mary, the mother of Jesus, in the Roman Catholic Church and makes a good point concerning the theory of a married Mary Magdalene. He says:

I would add also that with the very early veneration of Mary, the mother of Jesus, in Roman Catholicism, largely out of a desire to have a quasi-divine female figure along with God the Father, had Jesus ever been married, such a woman could scarcely have disappeared without a historical trace. She would have been celebrated and venerated instead, especially in the very strands of Catholicism that *The Da Vinci Code* pit against the revelation of "the truth" of Jesus' marriage.

I agree; the reason there is no trace is that Mary was not married to Jesus. In my office

47

there are thirty-eight volumes of early church documents, each of several hundred pages, double columns, in small print. The fact that out of all of this material, only two texts can be brought forward as even ancient candidates for the theory shows how utterly unlikely it is.

What About Mary Magdalene Outside the Bible?

In regard to all the texts we have surveyed one observation needs to be made: there is no clear text outside the Bible indicating that Jesus was married or that Mary Magdalene was His wife. This matches what is in the New Testament. Our survey of these extrabiblical texts, with their difficult images, shows that Mary was seen as one of the early witnesses to the Resurrection, something the New Testament usage also shows. We shall come back to these passages when we discuss Codes 4 and 5. For now, we are interested only in what they affirm about *The Da Vinci Code*'s key idea that Jesus was married to Mary Magdalene.

These texts, whatever their ultimate character, do not affirm that. They do not even make an argument for Jesus being married.

Was Mary Magdalene a Prostitute?

None of the texts we have surveyed referred to Mary Magdalene as a prostitute. The idea is popular in some sections of the church and in the culture at large. So where did this tradition about her arise?

The first mention of Mary as a prostitute comes from a homily (or sermon) delivered by Pope Gregory the Great in A.D. 591. In all likelihood, this notion resulted from confusion concerning passages in the gospels of Luke and John.

In the midst of Jesus' ministry, an unnamed sinful woman anointed Him at the house of Simon the leper (Luke 7:36–50). The text does not call this unnamed woman a prostitute, but the assumption is that her sin involves sexual promiscuity. Prostitution is the most likely activity, but she could have been an adulteress.

The next text is Luke 8:1–3, where Mary Magdalene is named. She is called one who was the beneficiary of an exorcism by Jesus. There is no mention of her anointing anyone.

A third text is John 12:1–8. Mary of Bethany anointed Jesus in public at the end of His ministry six days before Passover.

Here is one mystery we can solve quickly

49

and move on. Virtually all scholars now agree about it. Luke 8:1–3 introduces Mary of Magdala as if she is a new character. Luke made no effort to connect Mary to the previous scene in his gospel involving the sinful woman who anointed Jesus in the middle of His ministry. It would have been very easy to say she was the woman who had just anointed Jesus, but he did not.

So why would someone say she was a prostitute? If someone equated the unnamed woman in Luke 7 with the Mary of Magdala in Luke 8 (link and confusion #1) and then connected that reference to Mary with Mary of Bethany (link and confusion #2), one could suggest that Mary of Magdala was a prostitute. In addition, the two similar anointings (in Luke 7 and in John 12) make such a link look plausible. But there is no Mary in the first anointing, and the timing of the two anointings differs enough that one should not equate them. One clue is uncovered: the association of Mary Magdalene with prostitution is very unlikely.

What Can We Say About Mary of Magdala?

We know that Mary Magdalene was a faithful disciple, a witness to the cross,

50

burial, and resurrection of Jesus. She was not a prostitute. Some later texts suggest that she was privileged to receive revelation from Jesus. We will examine the significance of her exact role later, but for now we know she was not married to Jesus. At least there is no evidence in the Bible or outside it that says she was married to Jesus. A major element of the novel is in trouble. The first Da Vinci Code is broken. The theory that Mary and Jesus were married lacks evidence tied to passages associated with Mary Magdalene.

But what is the evidence like from Jesus' side? Is there any evidence to suggest that He was married to any other woman, much less Mary? We turn to Code 2. Is there a secret that unlocks whether Jesus was married?

Code 2

WAS JESUS MARRIED?

The well-known, liberal Jesus scholar John Dominic Crossan was asked on Beliefnet.com whether Jesus was married. He began his sarcastic reply this way:

> There is an ancient and venerable principle of biblical exegesis [interpretation] which states that if it looks like a duck, walks like a duck, and quacks like a duck, it must be a camel in disguise. So let's apply that to whether or not Jesus was married. There is no evidence that Jesus was married (looks like a duck), multiple indications that he was not (walks like a duck), and no early texts suggesting wife or children (quacks like a duck) . . . so he must be an incognito bridegroom (camel in disguise).

At one level, to hear the question about whether Jesus was married strikes one as odd. Almost everyone holds that Jesus was so dedicated to His ministry that He remained single.

A Look at the Claim That Jesus Was Married

Although I agree with Crossan's assessment, to reply with humor or to simply dismiss the question about whether Jesus was married is not an adequate response. Some have given reasons why they think Jesus was married. In *The Da Vinci Code*, the Opus Dei attempts to cover up the "fact" that Jesus had a family and children in order to protect His claim to deity. In the novel the Opus Dei is a secret church society whose goal is to protect the church by any means. The novel argues the case for Jesus' marriage on two primary bases: (1) that it was un-Jewish to be unmarried (p. 245), and (2) that according to Gnostic texts, Jesus kissed Mary on the mouth, and the apostles were jealous of His special relationship (pp. 246–47). To make the study complete, I shall include other arguments, from outside the novel, often brought forward to establish that Jesus was married.

At the start I must say several things. (1) There is no evidence anywhere that explicitly indicates Jesus was married. (2) One of the few things on which a vast majority of liberal and conservative Jesus scholars agree is that Jesus was single. Crossan in his

53

Beliefnet.com piece did not feel the need to defend the case that Jesus was single. To him, it was that obvious. It is such an unusual situation in the study of Jesus for scholars of all persuasions to agree — when it happens, one should note it. The agreed-upon point is quite likely valid. (3) On the other hand, we have no explicit text declaring that Jesus was single. (4) On several occasions, it would have been easy for writers in the New Testament to say that Jesus was married if that was the case. This issue is also the burden of the investigation at the end of this chapter. (5) Even if Jesus had been married, it would not have had the devastating effect on Jesus' claim of divinity that the conspiracy view alleges.

Let's deal with the last point first. Jesus did many things that underscored His genuine humanity. He ate, thirsted, slept, tired, lived, and died. His everyday life was that of a normal human existence. His life was exceptional because of His relationship with God, His access to divine power, and His resurrection. One of the most basic beliefs of Christian faith is that Jesus was 100 percent human. So if He had been married and fathered children, His marital relationship and His parenthood would not theoretically undercut His divinity but would have been reflections of His complete humanity. Had Jesus been married, there was no need to cover it up. The whole rationale for covering up any supposed relationship has no basis in theology. Had Jesus been married, theoretically He still could have been and done all He did. This leads us to the major question: What evidence is there that Jesus was or was not married?

1. Mary Traveled with Jesus

Let's now consider the reasoning brought forward to make the claim that Jesus was married. The major evidence is the text in Luke 8:1–3 that we reviewed earlier. Three women traveled with Jesus and supported His ministry team. The claim is that to travel with men or to live alongside men in such a way was unusual in the culture — a true claim. The inference then is made that Mary and Jesus must have been married for it to have been an acceptable situation.

To begin to make such a deduction, however, we must wed this text and idea to additional later texts. Those texts say that Jesus had a special relationship with Mary Magdalene. Such a link is required because Luke 8:1–3 notes three women: Susanna, Joanna, and Mary Magdalene. If traveling

55

with the disciples in ministry suggests a marriage, then one would have to link Mary exclusively to Jesus, which Luke 8:1–3 does not do.

2. Other Texts Show That Jesus and Mary Had a "Special" Relationship

Yet a second suggestion comes to complete the argument. It is that texts from a century or more later than Luke indicate that Mary had a special relationship with Jesus that *could* point to marriage. This is the argument to which the novel appeals. The texts are the later Gnostic-like texts, the books of Philip and Mary of Magdala, which we noted in exploring who Mary Magdalene was. They include the ideas that she was a companion of someone (perhaps Jesus) since she was in the traveling party and that Jesus kissed her (but where or in what context is not known).

No passage in these books actually states that Jesus was married. The best that can be brought forward is that Jesus loved Mary more than He did others and that there was some unclear display of affection. No statement even raises the issue whether the information in these later texts is accurate, that is, whether the sources of such information are credible. The claims assume the accuracy of these texts. Even if the texts are accurate, the claims in these texts fall far short of showing that Jesus was married (as we saw in examining Code 1).

There is an irony in the use of such extrabiblical texts. It is that some people raise questions and doubts about some of the biblical gospel material because they regard it as prejudicial. (The belief is that the biblical texts reflect the view of the later "winners" in church history, so we cannot completely trust these sources. These biblical texts deny the variety of Christianity that existed in the first few centuries.) Yet authors writing more than a century later, operating on what seems to be the fringe of Christianity, are treated as if they speak truth — no questions asked. Do these texts lack a perspective and prejudice? Might they also distort the facts if the texts of the "winners" do? What makes such texts immune from examination? We shall return to this point in more detail in Codes 4 and 5. For now we need to remember two things: (1) these texts, even if true, never claim Jesus was married, and (2) these texts need to be subjected to the same critical eye that some give the more ancient, biblical material. It's likely that these texts never explicitly link Jesus and Mary as husband and wife because their authors shared the common knowledge that Jesus was not married.

A second, independent argument for the marriage of Mary Magdalene and Jesus appeals to the scene of the sinful woman anointing Him in Luke 7:36–50. The argument is that this scene would not have been so offensive if the woman anointing Him had been His wife. This approach is fraught with problems we have already covered. The anointing woman of Luke 7 is not to be identified with Mary in Luke 8. More than that, the woman's act as portrayed in Luke 7 was seen as offensive. As a result, the remark by the Jewish host was that if Jesus knew what sort of woman she was, He would not have allowed the anointing (Luke 7:39). How could such an argument apply if the woman was His wife?

To raise this text in this light, one has to cast doubt on the way that Luke 7 presents it. But if this text were so inaccurate in its portrayal, then how could the text give us anything of value for our question? Either Luke 7 is true — and it is clear that Jesus was not married to the woman who anointed Him — or the text is so inaccurate that it cannot be used to help us with the question. I think the text is accurate. It fits

58

the frequent portrayal of Jesus as being open to and accepting of sinners who seek Him out. Either way, Luke 7 does not support the idea that Jesus was married.

3. Jesus As a Good Jew Would Be Married

Proponents of Jesus being a married man make a third argument, and the novel also appeals to it: because Jesus was a teacher and functioned like a rabbi, He would have followed Jewish custom and married.

Two factors make this argument weak. First, Jesus was not technically a rabbi, and He did not portray Himself as one. The apostles called Him rabbi in Matthew and Mark because He was their teacher, not because He held an official Jewish role. In fact, when Luke described Jesus' role, he used the term *teacher* rather than *rabbi*. The Jews asked Jesus by what authority He did certain things because He did not occupy any official position within Judaism that would have permitted Him to act as He did within the temple (Mark 11:28). Jesus was not a rabbi nor did He always act like one. As far as the Jewish leaders were concerned, Jesus had no recognized official role within Judaism.

Second, Jesus' teaching of the kingdom's

call to be eunuchs appears to be rooted in His commitment and example not to be married (Matt. 19:10–12). Why would Jesus issue such a statement, acknowledge it as a demanding calling, and not follow it? Some of the rationale for the Roman Catholic Church's later view that priests should not be married is rooted in the view that Jesus was not married. We shall consider in detail this idea that it is un-Jewish for Jewish men to be single in the next chapter on Code 3.

4. An Initial Cultural Response: Jewish Men and Women Together at Qumran

What of the unusual Jewish cultural practice of women, such as Mary Magdalene, living alongside men? There was a precedent of sorts at Qumran, better known as the community of the Dead Sea Scrolls, a Jewish separatist enclave that resided near the Dead Sea from the mid-second century B.C. to several decades after the time of Christ. This community raises the possibility of people living together for religious reasons and yet refraining from marriage.

We know that Jewish women and men lived in the wilderness, some apparently in a celibate state as a reflection of their commitment to God's kingdom. There is indication that some men in this community took on a pledge of celibacy because women lived near them in a separate community. Crossan puts it this way:

> We also know that a profound utopian theology was the basis for the lifestyle of the Essenes, who lived in Jesus' time. In order, as their Qumran Rule of the Community puts it, "to bring about truth, justice and uprightness on earth" the successful sect member enters God's Community by "the placing of his possessions in common." Judging by their Dead Sea Scrolls and their carefully buried skeletons, those Qumran Essenes were an all-male group living in communal celibacy, ritual purity, and eschatological holiness — living in a sense like angels, with heaven already touching earth.

Crossan notes what is well known about the cemetery finds in the community: the remains are strictly male. However, just outside the periphery of the main cemetery are remains of a few women and children. This cemetery evidence is noted by Qumran scholar Geza Vermes in *The Dead Sea Scrolls in English* (p. 18). Many Essenes were known for their emphasis on celibacy (Josephus, *Antiquities* 18.1.5.20–21; *Jewish War* 2.8.2.121–22; Philo, *Hypothetica* 11.14–17).

A passage from Josephus, the famous first-century Jewish historian, also testifies to celibacy in discussing the practice of the Essenes, the probable Jewish sect that inhabited Qumran:

It also deserves our admiration, how much they [the Essenes] exceed all other men that addict themselves to virtue, and this in righteousness; and indeed to such a degree, that as it has never appeared among any other man, neither Greeks nor barbarians, no, not for a little time, so has it endured a long while among them. This is demonstrated by that institution of theirs which will not suffer anything to hinder them from having all things in common; so that a rich man enjoys no more of his own wealth than he who has nothing at all. There are about four thousand men that live in this way, and neither marry wives, nor are desirous to keep servants; as thinking the latter tempts men to be unjust, and the former gives the handle to domestic quarrels; but as they live by

62

themselves, they minister one to another. (*Antiquities* 18.1.5.20–21)

We shall return to the rationale for these Jewish practices in the next chapter, for they provide a clue to the religious and cultural environment of the first century. For now, we need to appreciate that some Jews did not view marriage as an obligation and chose celibacy as a sign of piety. For those at Qumran, remaining single was about single-minded dedication to God. Paul exhibited a similar attitude in 1 Corinthians 7 when he advised the people not to marry because of the nature of the times; nevertheless if one did marry, he said, it was not sin. The point is that mutual ministry could take place across gender lines. It was unusual in the culture, but it would not mean that one had to be married to do so or that celibacy could not be practiced.

The Case for Jesus As a Single Man

Most scholars have long believed that Jesus was single, and we will examine three arguments supporting that belief. No early Christian text we possess, either biblical or extrabiblical, indicates the presence of a wife during His ministry, His crucifixion, or after His resurrection. Whenever texts mention Jesus' family, they refer to His mother, brothers and sisters but never to a wife. Furthermore, there is no hint that He was widowed. To paraphrase Crossan, "If it walks like a duck and quacks like a duck, it must be a duck!"

1. Mary Was Never Tied to Any Male When She Was Named

The first argument for Jesus being single takes us back to passages from Matthew, Mark, Luke, and John where Mary Magdalene was named (Matt. 27:55–56; Mark 15:40–41; Luke 8:2; John 19:25). In these texts other women listed were connected to *prominent or well-known* males in their lives. It was an important clue, and here is where that clue applies. If Mary had been married to Jesus, this listing would be the place to mention it, as had been done with other women who were connected to sons or husbands. No listing of Mary Magdalene or any other woman does this to say that Jesus was married.

Matthew, Mark, Luke, and John were written within a generation or two of Jesus' life. Most scholars date the last biblical gospel, John, to the A.D. nineties. There was no "plot" yet to keep the details of Jesus' life

64

a secret nor was there an established precedent that ministers might not have the right to marry. Later in 1 Corinthians 9:4–6, Paul, a minister of the gospel, believed he had a right to certain things — such as marriage — rights that he did not use but that were possible for him.

2. A Minister's Right to Marry Was Cited Without Reference to Jesus

First Corinthians 9:4–6 may be the most important text for this topic. It reads, "Do we not have the right to financial support? Do we not have the right to the company of a believing wife, like the other apostles and the Lord's brothers and Cephas? Or do only Barnabas and I lack the right not to work?" Paul noted in this aside that the apostles, the Lord's brothers, and Cephas (Peter) had the right to a wife. In other words, they had every right to be married. It would have been simple for Paul to add that Jesus was married — had He been. Such a point would have sealed his argument, but he did not make that point. Some might object by suggesting that Paul cited only people who were alive. But the response to such an objection is that Paul was discussing precedent and rights. To raise the example of what someone did would be possible and logical, *had Jesus had such a status*. The conclusion is that Paul did not make the point because he could not make such a point.

This 1 Corinthians 9 passage shows that the church was not embarrassed to reveal that its leaders were married — or to suggest that they had the right to be. The same would have been true of Jesus if He had been married. In fact, had Jesus been married, there would have been no better place for Paul to say it than here. It would have clinched Paul's case that he also had the right to be married. Paul did not mention it because Jesus had not been married.

Some will reply that 1 Corinthians 7 could be made to make the same point in reverse. This entire chapter affirmed that remaining single is advised. Why did not Paul make the same point with Jesus here that one argues for in chapter 9 of 1 Corinthians? He could have well said that Jesus was single and made Him the example. That would have sealed Paul's point, but he did not say it. The point would be that such arguments from silence prove nothing.

The point is well taken, but a reasonable reply is possible. The difference in the two situations of 1 Corinthians 7 and 1 Corinthians 9 may well show that not all silence is equal when it comes to noting differences in

66

the nature of the evidence. Paul did not need to make a point about Jesus' singleness because it was well known, assumed, and not debated. More than that, and more important, Paul's view was not that one must be single, but that singleness was advisable. To bring up Jesus as the example would make the point about being single in too strong a manner. He wanted people to take seriously the option of remaining single, but he did not suggest that marriage was wrong. So he did not mention Jesus.

3. Jesus Showed No Special Concern for Mary Magdalene at the Cross

As we examine the scene of the cross, we see a third and final argument indicating that Jesus was single. At the cross many believing women, including Jesus' mother, gathered. If there was an occasion where family would be present, it was there as Jesus was dying. Yet no wife was described. Jesus was most concerned about His mother as He gave her into John's care (John 19:26–27). In addition, had Jesus been married, His wife would have been present with His mother to celebrate the Passover festival that brought them to Jerusalem during the time of Jesus' arrest. Once again, no wife was mentioned because there was no wife.

What Can We Say About Jesus Being Married?

The discussion surrounding whether Jesus was married has been particularly complex, but such is the case in investigating mysteries. Sometimes juries have to hear detailed testimony about DNA and double helixes, a topic they typically would not encounter in daily life. Sorting out whether Jesus was married requires careful examination of ancient texts and Jewish history, topics not typically part of everyday discussion.

It has long been believed by Christians and scholars that Jesus was single, and there are good reasons for this belief. When He was in ministry, there was no mention of a wife. When He was tried and crucified, there was no mention of a wife. After His death and resurrection, there was no mention of a wife. Jesus' family members — His mother, brothers, and sisters — were mentioned more than once, but never a wife. Nor was there any indication that He was widowed.

This is not an argument from silence in the classic sense because there were numerous opportunities to make the point about Jesus being married — had He been.

The problem here is that where no marriage has occurred, silence will be the result! Other texts show that Jesus supported a single lifestyle for some of His followers, an example that seemed to include Him.

So our second code is broken. What is the likelihood that Jesus was married? The answer here is short — none. So how does one explain Jesus being single? That is the third code we need to investigate because it helps us to appreciate how first-century culture differed from our own culture and reinforces the idea that Jesus had a reason to be single, even though the novel claims that Jesus had to be married.

Code 3

WOULD BEING SINGLE
MAKE JESUS UN-JEWISH?

The charge is sometimes made that Jesus had to be married because He was Jewish. As noted in Code 2, *The Da Vinci Code* makes this claim in setting forth its case that Jesus virtually had to be married because He was Jewish (p. 245). In fact, the novel claims that Jewish custom condemned celibacy (p. 245); it would be unthinkable for a Jewish man to remain single. Jewish men generally regarded marriage as an obligation of being human. Genesis 1:28 gave humans the command to be fruitful and multiply so that marriage was seen as fulfilling a fundamental responsibility as one created by God. Marriage was certainly the rule and expectation for Jews.

By the first century, there were exceptions to the rule. We have already noted the famous passage from Josephus in *Antiquities* 18 where he described the unusual, celibate practice of the Essenes, whether at Qumran or anywhere else they might have lived. This is only one clue that marriage was not an ab-

70

solute requirement for a Jew.

Other Jewish Texts on Celibacy, Singleness, and Gender Relations

A second text in Josephus describes the Essenes. It appears in *Jewish War* 2.8.2.121–22. This work, written in the first century, explains two major conflicts in Jewish history: the Maccabean War of 167–164 B.C. and the fall of Jerusalem to Rome in A.D. 70. Josephus was explaining the makeup of the Jewish religious world during that period, so he spoke about one of the Jewish sects. The term *sect* does not have the negative connotation it possesses today in English; it means a distinguishable religious party, a subgroup within Judaism.

Here is the text:

These Essenes reject pleasures as an evil, but esteem continence, and the conquest over our passions, to be virtue. They neglect wedlock, but choose out other persons' children, while they are pliable, and fit for learning; and esteem them to be of their kindred, and form them according to their own manners. They do not absolutely deny the fitness of marriage, and the succession of man-

71

kind thereby continued; but they guard against the lascivious behavior of women, and are persuaded that none of them preserve their fidelity to one man.

The people in that community of Jews were very hesitant about getting married and were concerned, based on religious grounds, about sexual relationships. Although celibacy was not an absolute requirement according to this text, it was encouraged. The danger of infidelity in marriage drove them to be careful about marriage.

Such an attitude about marriage and fidelity was not unusual in Judaism. A second-century B.C. book of Jewish wisdom, *Sirach*, which reads similarly to Proverbs, has many warnings about marriage and women. For example, *Sirach* 9:8 reads, "Turn away your eyes from a shapely woman, and do not gaze at beauty belonging to another; many have been seduced by a woman's beauty, and by it passion is kindled like a fire."

Such pious Jews took adultery seriously:

The one who sins against his marriage bed
says to himself, "Who can see me?

72

Darkness surrounds me, the walls hide
me,
and no one sees me. Why should I
worry?
The Most High will not remember
sins."
His fear is confined to human eyes
and he does not realize that the eyes
of the Lord
are ten thousand times brighter than
the sun;
they look upon every aspect of
human behavior
and see into hidden corners.
Before the universe was created, it was
known to him,
and so it is since its completion.
This man will be punished in the
streets of the city,
and where he least suspects it, he will
be seized.
So it is with a woman who leaves her
husband
and presents him with an heir by
another man. (*Sirach* 23:18–22)

This text makes it quite clear that the
pious regarded marriage as sacred. The
sacred nature of this relationship was not to
be violated. It is often said, and rightly so,

that some of the ancients were quite nervous about sexuality. They sensed its power and were very cautious about it. In fact, the most pious were willing to steer clear of marriage altogether.

There is one other text about the Essenes' celibacy, written by a first-century Jewish philosopher-historian named Philo, who lived in Egypt. He wrote about the Essenes in the book of *Hypothetica* 11.14–17. Be warned that this text is not politically correct when it comes to its description of women. It is not easy reading for our modern culture, but it reveals a concern among the pious of this era. This text reads:

> Perceiving with more than ordinary acuteness and accuracy, what is alone or at least above all other things calculated to dissolve such associations, they repudiate marriage; and at the same time they practice continence in an eminent degree; for no one of the Essenes ever marries a wife, because woman is a selfish creature and one addicted to jealousy in an immoderate degree, and terribly calculated to agitate and overturn the natural inclinations of a man, and to mislead him by her continual tricks; for as she is always studying deceitful

speeches and all other kinds of hypocrisy, like an actress on the stage, when she is alluring the eyes and ears of her husband, she proceeds to cajole his predominant mind after the servants have been deceived.

And again, if there are children she becomes full of pride and all kinds of license in her speech, and all the obscure sayings which she previously meditated in irony in a disguised manner she now begins to utter with audacious confidence; and becoming utterly shameless she proceeds to acts of violence, and does numbers of actions of which every one is hostile to such associations; for the man who is bound under the influence of the charms of a woman, or of children, by the necessary ties of nature, being overwhelmed by the impulses of affection, is no longer the same person towards others, but is entirely changed, having, without being aware of it, become a slave instead of a free man.

This now is the enviable system of life of these Essenes, so that not only private individuals but even mighty kings, admiring the men, venerate their sect, and increase their dignity and majesty in a still higher degree by their approbation and by the honors which they confer on them.

Do not misunderstand. I have not highlighted this text because I agree with what it expresses. Rather, it shows that among some pious Jews, there was an enormous concern for how the genders could and should relate to each other. It proves that not all Jews insisted on being married. In fact, some pious Jews tried to avoid it.

Thus, it is not a given that Jesus as a Jew would seek to be married. Even more important, it would not be a sign of shame to be single. The Essenes, though limited in numbers, were actually respected by many Jews for the depth of their religious conviction. Here again is the judgment of Josephus in *Antiquities* 18.1.5.20: "It also deserves our admiration, how much they exceed all other men that addict themselves to virtue, and this in righteousness; and indeed to such a degree, that as it has never appeared among any other man, neither Greeks nor barbarians, no, not for a little time, so has it endured a long while among them." In other words, many Jews admired their desire and ability to live in such a disciplined manner. It was not shameful or un-Jewish to live an unmarried

76

life as a Jewish man in the first century. These texts are the clues that show such an assertion to be false.

Jesus, Singleness, and Gender

We can never overlook a basic fact about Jesus: He did not follow the culture; He often cut a distinctive path. It seems that on the issue of sexuality Jesus did the same. Jesus did not reflect the negative, isolationist attitude toward women that these pious Jewish texts suggested. On the other hand, there is evidence, some of it already noted, suggesting that He urged caution in matters of sexuality. We look at such concerns here.

We already noted Matthew 19:10–12 where Jesus argued that some should be "eunuchs" for the kingdom as an indication of their dedication to it. Jesus appeared to be an example of such dedication in His own life. Another possible explanation for His singleness was the itinerant nature of His ministry. Being always on the move was not a lifestyle conducive to marriage or a family life.

On the other hand, Jesus did not hesitate to involve women or engage them in His ministry in ways that would have been offensive to some in the culture who wanted to segregate women more. Some of these texts have been referenced to make other points. For example, Luke 8:1–3 indicates that women were a part of the traveling entourage with Jesus. That Jesus did not hesitate to accept the offer of honor from women in public is seen in Luke 7:36–50 and John 12:1–8, when women anointed Him in public. In both cases, others were surprised that He accepted the action, but He did. John 4 records a scene where Jesus spoke in public with a woman from Samaria, an action that surprised His disciples, given the fact it took place in public. All of this shows that Jesus related directly to women in ways that fell outside the expectations of most in the culture.

The late second-century A.D. Jewish text called the Mishnah is the written collection of Jewish oral law. It discussed how men should relate to women in public. *Qiddushin* 4.14 of this text reads, "Whoever has business with women should not be alone with women." In *Avoth* 1.5, the text gives the opinion of one rabbi, Jose, son of Johanan, who said, "And don't talk too much with women." The rationale, as this text later suggests, was that such chatter brings trouble to oneself, it was better to spend time studying Torah, and such chatter leads one into becoming an heir of Gehenna (i.e., hell). Jesus' willingness to engage the Samaritan woman alone in public falls very much outside such limitations.

In fact, Jesus' accepting of women as disciples fell outside the scope of some rabbinic views. In the Mishnah again, one can consider *Berachah* 3.3. The following is said about the exemption of women from certain Jewish practices as well as what they should do. It reads, "Women, slaves, and minors are exempt from the recitation of the Shema and from [the obligation to wear] phylacteries, but are obligated to the [recitation of] the prayer, and to [post] a mezuzah and [to recite] the blessing over the meal." Reciting the Shema involved the daily recitation of Deuteronomy 6:4, which was a declaration of recognition that there is only one God. It was one of the most basic practices of Judaism. Phylacteries are little summaries of Torah that the most faithful Jews wore on the forehead. A mezuzah is a similar summary that was posted on one's house. Women were exempt from certain basic religious practices, an indication that they were not seen to have the same religious obligations as men.

There is another example of women being

limited in worship. The Feast of Tabernacles celebrates the exodus of Israel from Egypt and God's protection of and provision for Israel in the wilderness. Part of this feast is that celebrants must live in booths for a week, depicting the mobile character of the time in the wilderness with all of its risks. Women were not to live in booths for the week of celebration as the men did. These Mishnaic texts include the rulings of a second pious Jewish group, the rabbis, distinct from the Essenes. The rabbis constituted a major party of Judaism. They showed much concern about how a Jew should relate to women, and they argued for some gender distinction during a time just after the days of Jesus. With regard to such practices, most scholars hold that what the rabbis say in the Mishnah also reflected Jewish views in Jesus' time, as the book of *Sirach* also suggests. Most pious Jews in the first century handled gender, women, and marriage very differently from the way most people do in our time.

What did Jesus do? When it came to engaging women, Jesus operated in a different manner than much of official or pious Judaism, accepting their engagement with and their honor of Him. Jesus modeled balance. He had respect for religious commitment that resulted in His being single. Because of His respect for women, He treated them with esteem and received them as participants in God's plan. In all of this Jesus' practice was distinct from the frequent practice of other pious Jews.

In regard to marriage, Jesus argued strongly for fidelity. Jesus stated, "It was said, 'Whoever divorces his wife must give her a legal document.' But I say to you that everyone who divorces his wife, except for immorality, makes her commit adultery, and whoever marries a divorced woman commits adultery" (Matt. 5:31–32). The following verses (5:33–37) dealt with keeping oaths and letting a yes mean yes. So marriage was a solemn vow to Jesus, something to be honored and kept before God (note also Matthew 19:1–12; Mark 10:1–12). In respecting the sanctity of marriage, Jesus followed Jewish views.

What Can We Say About Jesus, Singleness, and Gender?

We have broken a third code. Jesus could well be single and fit into the practice of pious Jews. Not every Jew had to be married. There were times when the virtue of remaining single was followed by some and

81

respected by other Jews. There were good religious reasons why some Jews did not marry, most often out of intense religious dedication. Some also remained single for reasons of practicality given the nature of their chosen ministry. Other reasons might not be so compelling, but those other reasons help us to see the sensitive nature of gender for many in the first century. This provides an important backdrop for our later treatment of the role of women in the earliest church, a topic that we will cover in Code 6.

Yet as we explored some Jewish attitudes toward gender and engaging women in public, we saw clearly that Jesus did not follow strict Jewish practice. There was precedent for Jewish men to remain single, so Jesus' singleness wasn't un-Jewish; He would not have been condemned for such an approach to Jewish life. On the other hand, Jesus showed in other areas that He was willing to go against cultural convention so that even if it had been counter to Jewish practice, such a reason would not have stopped Jesus if He saw God's will being realized in going another way. Either way, there is good cultural precedent, as well as good evidence, to see that Jesus was single. We also sense that when it came to affirming women, Jesus did not follow the culture's limitations on them.

But where do we stand now in our investigation? In sum, it was not un-Jewish for Jesus to be single. Marriage was not a necessary step for Jesus to take to have cultural credibility in the Jewish context of His ministry. We have shown that (1) Jesus was not married, (2) Mary Magdalene was not His (secret) wife, and (3) singleness could be understood and appreciated by other Jews around Jesus. These conclusions reveal the fallacy of the core claim of *The Da Vinci Code* about Jesus being married to Mary. The novel is not well grounded in its historical claims and assumptions.

Taking Stock of Where the Investigation Is Leading

The novel does not stop here in its claims, however. It is not content merely to discuss Jesus and Mary Magdalene. It goes on to say things about early church history, the Bible, and the extrabiblical sources we have been examining. Investigations of mysteries and codes often open up new and fresh paths. We come to such a fork in our road here. The novel makes claims about texts and where they came from, who made them important or expendable, and why certain texts should or should not be considered as reflecting the standard that helps to explain Jesus and the Christian faith. We have to consider the novel's claims about the sources of such information. This detour is necessary to evaluate what we uncover from the texts the novel affirms.

In an investigation, one must pay attention to the information brought to light and the nature of the source of such information. So two issues need attention.

First, there is Code 4 or the nature of some of the "newly discovered" gospels. What kind of theology and spirituality did they teach? Are these texts reflective of Christianity as it was in its earliest period? Are they a "new way" to see Jesus? These gospels and related texts are the focus of our next chapter.

Second, we need to consider how the New Testament books became a part of our Bible. Exactly how and when did that happen for the Gospels? Was the New Testament put together almost three hundred years after the time of Christ as *The Da Vinci Code* argues? Are the four Gospels too distant in their reception to be of value to us in explaining who Jesus was and is? The examination of how the four Gospels were received into the church is the topic of Code 5.

We turn to the "secret" gospels, sometimes called the Gnostic gospels. Everyone loves to uncover secrets.

Code 4

DO THE SO-CALLED SECRET, GNOSTIC
GOSPELS HELP US UNDERSTAND JESUS?

One of the more interesting claims in *The Da
Vinci Code* appears on page 231. It comes
from Teabing, a character who is full of opinions about Christianity that are critical of the
church and that possess conspiratorial impli-
cations. Here he claims that there were
"more than *eighty* gospels" considered for the
New Testament, but that only four were
chosen. This may be the most misleading
statement of "fact" in the entire novel.

Teabing's statement is so misleading because there were not more than eighty
gospel documents. For example, *The Nag
Hammadi Library*, published in English in
1977, consisted of forty-five separate titles
— and not all of them were gospels. In fact,
it names five separate works as gospels:
Truth, *Thomas*, *Philip*, *Egyptians*, and *Mary*.
The collection of *The Gnostic Scriptures* by
Bentley Layton has just short of forty works,
three of which bear the title *gospel* and
overlap with the Nag Hammadi list. In fact,

86

most of these works were not gospels. The most generous count of extrabiblical documents appears in Harvard Professor Helmut Koester's *Introduction to the New Testament.* That count stands at sixty, excluding the twenty-seven books in the New Testament. However, a vast majority of these works were not gospels.

The allusion here in part is to what has been called the Gnostic materials. Many of these manuscripts surfaced when Muhammed Ali (not the famous boxer) stumbled across a jar of texts while digging in a cave. As was the case with ancient discoveries of now famous texts, the surfacing of the ancient treasure happened almost by accident, not by design. This discovery took place in 1945 at a location known as Nag Hammadi in the deserts of Egypt. Knowledge of groups now called the Gnostics, along with their beliefs, and perhaps parts of their texts are found in the writings of many church fathers, such as Irenaeus (ca. 130–200), Hippolytus (ca. 170–236), and Tertullian (ca. 160–after 220). These church fathers lived in the second and third centuries and played a major role in describing what many in the early church believed. One of them, Epiphanius (ca. 310–403), in a work he described as "a medicine chest" against heresies, speaks of "practicing Gnostics" giving us the name for this teaching. The earlier work of Irenaeus confirms this naming by noting in the preface to his *Against Heresies* that he writes against those who draw away many under a pretense of knowledge. These fathers were very critical of the Gnostics, insisting that their teachings were at odds with apostolic preaching and teaching. So elements of these doctrines taught in these newly discovered materials, and maybe even a few of these writings, are not as "secret" as some currently seeking to dramatize their nature have suggested. The views of such groups have been known for well over a millennium. They are "ancient" history.

What was new was that now, rather than learning about these other groups and their beliefs through the writing of those who were critical of the Gnostics, these writers could speak for themselves from their own documents. These texts were dramatic proof that in the second and third centuries some who took on the name "Christian" had views that differed from what is typically thought of as Christian. As a result, much study has been given to these documents, and they have been heavily debated.

The Gnostic materials and other ancient

related texts are important finds. I speak of the Gnostics and their relatives because scholars debate what Gnosticism is, who Gnostic Christians were, and whether all these newly discovered materials should be called Gnostic. These technical debates need not detain us. We just need to understand the general character of these beliefs, whatever name they receive. That is our goal in examining Code 4.

In the Nag Hammadi materials we find new, intriguing titles, some gospels and some not. Such titles include *Gospel of Thomas*, *Gospel of Philip*, *Gospel of Mary*, *Acts of John*, *Testimony of Truth*, *Pistis Sophia*, *Wisdom of Jesus Christ*, and many others. Their dates range from the second to the third century A.D., although a few works are alleged to be older or at least to reflect older views. This could be the case for some bits of this material, but not for most of it. The bulk of this material is a few generations removed from the foundations of the Christian faith, a vital point to remember when assessing the contents. Just what did these documents, which were not accepted into the canon of Scripture, teach? Furthermore, what kind of Christianity did they espouse?

The Beliefs Found in These Other Gospels and Their Related Texts

Whether one looks at these new documents or the early church teachers who were highly critical of them, four major theological issues and one underlying conviction drove the ancient debate. Thus, five features of these texts are the focus of our investigation. (1) The basic conviction underlying these four issues was that these documents reveal mysterious, new truth, the *gnosis* or knowledge. These texts are Gnostic because it is their most fundamental feature. These issues include (2) the teaching about God and the cosmological "worlds" associated with Him; (3) the person of Jesus, the work on the cross, and salvation; (4) the role of revelation, authority, and spirituality in defining the faith; and (5) to a lesser degree, the role of women.

With each theme our investigation will present what these works said. Remember that in different works we may meet a variety of views on particular points; these texts do not teach exactly the same thing. Yet even though there is a range of belief in such works, they hold certain things in common. And we are going to examine closely many of their shared emphases that appear distinct from the teachings of well-known Christian documents. (For readers interested in a sympathetic examination of these sources in more detail, the work by Elaine Pagels, *The Gnostic Gospels*, is a helpful, standard source.)

1. The Basic Theme Underlying These Texts: *Gnosis,* or Knowledge

Central to all elements of this view was the idea that some Christians had access to *mysteries* or advanced, exclusive teaching that other Christians did not possess. Many of these works elaborated on these "mysterious" features of the faith. The term *secret* fits well with this material, for it was special, in-house teaching given only to the few, the spiritual. Most of these secrets involved areas where the teaching distinguished itself from other public Christian teaching. These secrets and the inside understanding they produced were the *gnosis* or knowledge received by the beneficiaries of such revelation. This basic and shared feature causes most scholars to call these works Gnostic because they deal in special knowledge only for insiders.

For example, an obscure but important text was the *Apocalypse of Peter* 82:17–

83:15. The symbol (?) means that the translation at this particular point is not certain. If the meaning of all of the text's details is not immediately clear, do not be too concerned. We are interested in its most basic points. The text reads:

And he [the Savior] said to me [Peter], "Be strong, for you are the one to whom these mysteries have been given. To know them through revelation, that he whom they crucified is first-born, and the home of the demons, and the stoney vessel (?) in which they dwell of Elohim, of the cross which is under the Law. But he who stands near him is the living Savior, the first in him, whom they seized and released, who stands joyfully looking at those who did him violence, while they were divided among themselves. Therefore he laughs at their lack of perception, knowing that they are born blind. So then the one susceptible to suffering shall come, since the body is the substitute. But what they released was my incorporeal body. But I am the intellectual Spirit filled with radiant light. He whom you saw coming to me is our intellectual *Pleroma,* which unites perfect light with my Holy Spirit."

This text exhibits three key features of a direct, revelatory view for Gnostic-like views. First, there is reference to the *Pleroma,* the pure, heavenly, immaterial fullness that is truly and completely divine. This is the supreme God of these texts. Gnostic views held to a dualism, a radical opposition that taught that the world of ideas was a pure world, while the physical world was corrupt. The true God (often called the Incorruptible) was a part of this world of ideas and was light. He did not enter directly into the physical creation. Second, there is the distinction between the Savior's physical (corporeal) body that suffered on the cross and the true, incorporeal body that is pure light, which saw the Savior suffer. This second figure is the true Jesus for this group. Third, this entire teaching is a mystery; it is unique revelation that Peter has received from Jesus. This is the most basic characteristic of these texts. They are filled with mysteries now revealed, and only insiders have access to and can appreciate these mysteries. These insiders have "the knowledge," the *gnosis.*

This point stands in some contrast to the view of revelation in the texts that are now a part of the Bible. These biblical texts are recorded and given openly for all to consider.

Before the New Testament existed as documents, these respected Christian writings were read to the congregations. They held no claim to "insider" knowledge as the Gnostic-like texts did. Revelation was presented for all to consider, accept, or reject, while setting forth the benefits and consequences of such a deliberation. Neither was there dualism between pure knowledge and the creation as inherently corrupt. God's creation was good, although creation suffered from the fallenness of sin and its destructive effects. Knowing God meant seeing oneself the way God did and sensing the need for Him, not just getting access to secret knowledge.

2. God and the "Cosmological" Worlds Associated with Him

These groups' teaching about God and His relationship with the creation has a dualistic edge. (Remember that dualism means that two principles are harshly opposed to each other.) For these groups, there exists the eternal, supreme, transcendent Father who is utterly spiritual and has no contact with anything material. In opposition to Him is the Creator of the physical world, a fallen, wicked, arrogant being often called the *Demiurge,* or "maker," who falsely

94

believes himself to be the only god. These Gnostic or Gnostic-like groups demean and ridicule this imposter and the physical things associated with him because he does not acknowledge the Pure Father of the true immaterial world and because he is the craftsman of things material. Thus, this underling's understanding is deficient and ignorant.

The third-century document *Hypostasis of the Archons* introduces us to such teaching about God and the *Demiurge*. This text also shows the conflict between the "authorities" or "archons" and the Father of Truth. In *Hypostasis* 86:20–87:11, we find a particularly significant passage. The parentheses in this translation provide clarifying explanations or note references to biblical texts. Brackets mean that the text has a break and the translation is what is likely to have been present. The passage reads,

On account of the reality (hypostasis) of the authorities, (inspired) by the Spirit of the Father, the great apostle (Paul) — referring to the "authorities of the darkness" (Colossians 1:13) — told us that "our contest is not against flesh and [blood]; rather, the authorities of the universe and the spirits of wickedness"

(Ephesians 6:12). [I have] sent (you) this because you (sing.) inquire about the reality [of the] Authorities.

Their chief is blind; [because of his] Power and his ignorance [and his] arrogance he said with his [Power], "It is I who am God; there is none [apart from me]."

When he said this, he sinned against [the *Pleroma*]. And this speech got up to Incorruptibility; then there was a voice that came forth from Incorruptibility, saying, "You are mistaken, Samuel" — which is "god of the blind."

His thoughts became blind. And, having expelled his Power — that is, the blasphemy he had spoken — he pursued it down to Chaos and the Abyss, his mother, at the instigation of Pistis Sophia (Faith-Wisdom). And she established each of his offspring in conformity with its power — after the pattern of the realms that are above, for by starting from the invisible world the visible world was invented.

This text is hard to follow because of its conception of God. Here is a complex deity, existing in a series of worlds. There also is a conflict between multiple heavenly authorities. Most important to our discussion is that humanity is created by these "archons," according to the following text in 87:11–26.

These verses read,

As Incorruptibility looked down into the region of the waters, her image [Pistis Sophia] appeared in the Waters; and the Authorities of the Darkness became enamored of her. But they could not lay hold of that Image, which had appeared to them in the waters, because of their weakness – since beings that merely possess a soul cannot lay hold of those that possess a Spirit – ; for they were from Below, while it was from Above. This is why "Incorruptibility looked down into the regions [of the waters]": so that by the Father's will, she might bring Entirety into union with the Light. The rulers (Archons) laid plans and said, "Come, let us create a man that will be soil from the earth." They modeled their creature as one wholly of the earth.

After this, the soul-filled man lies lifeless on the ground. Only the *Pleroma* (the Incorruptible) sends the Spirit to indwell the man and give Adam life (88:10-15).

The material world and humanity were created as part of a fallen world from the beginning. The God of the highest realm provides the breath of spiritual life, but the creation primarily was the act of other beings. Here was a theology that had a distinct code for understanding the world. The creation of humanity was a group project of heaven and lesser forces.

How do we assess this doctrine of God? The Eastern Orthodox scholar Frederica Mathewes-Green has summarized the situation between more traditionally rooted Christians and those like the Gnostics when it came to religious experience, beliefs, and the confession expressed in the church creeds. In doing so, she gives a helpful overview of the Gnostic's view of God and creation. In the article "What Heresy?" published in *Books and Culture* (November–December 2003) she discusses religious experiences, how we share them, and the ancient debate between the Christians who affirmed a creed and the Gnostics, with their distinctive, complex view of God:

There is such a thing as self-deception, and confusion can bloom in unfamiliar spiritual realms. Though such experiences are indisputably beyond words,

98

after we have them we try to talk about them. We want to share them with others, and we want to check whether we simply flipped out. Say that it's like going to Paris. Everyone takes a photo of the Eiffel Tower. When we get home, we compare them; some snapshots are fuzzy and some from funny angles, but we can recognize them as depicting the same thing. The snaps don't capture the reality; nothing can; but they're OK as records.

The Creeds are photos everyone agreed on. They are minimal and crisply focused, not fancied-up. They are not a substitute for personal experience, but a useful guide for comparison, for discernment. If someone's snap shows King Kong climbing up the Tower, we can say, "Hey, you're off base there. Something's messing with your head." If Kong is wearing a lei and a paper party hat we might say, "Aw, now you're just making stuff up."

That's what early Christians said to the Gnostics. The problem wasn't the insistence that we can directly experience God. It was that the Gnostics' schemes of how to do this were so *wacky*. Preposterous stories about creation, angels, demons, and spiritual hierarchies multiplied like mushrooms. (Even some Christians, like Origen and Clement of Alexandria, dabbled in these fields.) The version attributed to Valentinus, the best-known Gnostic, is typical. Valentinus supposedly taught a hierarchy of spiritual beings called "aeons." One of the lowest aeons, Sophia, fell and gave birth to the *Demiurge,* the God of the Hebrew Scriptures. This evil Demiurge created the visible world, which was a bad thing, because now we pure spirits are all tangled up in fleshy bodies. Christ was an aeon who took possession of the body of the human Jesus, and came to free us from the prison of materiality.

"Us," by the way, didn't mean everybody. Not all people have a divine spark within, just intellectuals; "gnosis," by definition, concerns what you know. Some few who are able to grasp these insights could be initiated into deeper mysteries. Ordinary Christians, who lacked sufficient brainpower, could only attain the *Demiurge*'s middle realm. Everyone else was doomed. Under Gnosticism, there was no hope of salvation for most of the human race.

Mathewes-Green's major point is that there were great differences between the more traditionally rooted Christians who looked back to the apostolic era and those claiming access to special knowledge. Theologically and conceptually the move from one camp to another was like leaping over a canyon.

Mathewes-Green's description of the Gnostic Valentinus's views comes from the church father Irenaeus and his second-century work, *Against Heresies* 1.11.1. It might be better to continue to let the Gnostic works make the case for the view they defend.

Here is a text from the *Apocryphon of John* 2:9–25, another second-century work that highlighted secret revelation. This text also gives a glimpse of the view of God among this group. Jesus addressed John as Jesus was explaining who He was. It reads:

He said to me, "John, Jo[h]n, why do you doubt, and why are you afraid? You are not unfamiliar with this image, are you? — that is, do not [be] timid! I am the one who [is with all of you] always. I [am the Father]; I am the Mother; I am the Son. I am the undefiled and incorruptible one. Now [I have come to teach you] what is [and what was] and what will come to [pass], that [you may know the] things that are not revealed [and those which are revealed, and to teach you] concerning the [unwavering race of] perfect [Man]. Now, [therefore, lift up] your [face that] you may [receive] the things that I [shall teach you] today, [and] may [tell them to your] fellow spirits who [are from] the [unwavering] race of the perfect Man."

This text highlights the mystery feature prevalent in these texts. Here God is a complex figure, consisting of Father, Mother, and Son. Many of these texts portrayed God as a dyad, with the divine mother as part of the original couple. Irenaeus, writing in *Against Heresies* 1.11.1, complained about the view of a major teacher, Valentinus, who spoke of God as a dyad. Valentinus believed that God consisted in two parts. In one part, God was the Ineffable, the Depth, the Primal Father; and in the other, Grace, Silence, the Womb, and "Mother of the All." This Grace and Silence was the feminine complement of God, and her womb received the seed of the Ineffable Source to bring forth the emanations of divine being.

The recognition of the divine feminine

102

distinguishes Gnosticism from the Jewish and Christian presentations of God. The Judeo-Christian tradition argued that God lacks gender. In fact, males *and* females were made in God's image (Gen. 1:27). The closest that these other Jewish and Christian views of God came to such feminine understandings appears in the metaphorical portrayal of Wisdom as a female (Prov. 8).

Lest this incorporation of the divine feminine be understood as suggesting these Gnostics viewed females in a positive light or as equals, one should note the following text from *Gospel of Thomas* 114: "Simon Peter said to them [the disciples], 'Let Mary leave us, for women are not worthy of Life.' Jesus said, 'I myself shall lead her, in order to make her male, so that she too may become a living spirit, resembling you males. For every woman who will make herself male will enter the Kingdom of Heaven.' " This *Thomas* text is worth remembering when we discuss the role of women portrayed in these direct revelatory texts.

It is not clear that the Gnostics had a politically correct understanding of gender centuries before the rest of us. Something else is taking place. The secret of deity is not so mysterious after all; the process of creation is made in humanity's image and likeness. How different is this picture of Creation from the poetic renderings of Genesis 1–2, where God alone speaks and Creation takes place or where God alone forms and gives life.

In short, the view of God found in these texts is very different from that in the biblical texts of the Judeo-Christian tradition. In these texts, we see a distant God, too transcendent to get his hands dirty with humanity, working through emissaries. In the New Testament, we see God becoming flesh and entering into our suffering to the point of taking it upon Himself for our behalf. The difference is huge.

3. The Person of Jesus, the Work on the Cross, and Salvation

Another distinctive feature of Gnosticism involved how Jesus was understood in His person, suffering, and work of salvation. Here we consider three texts. The first is *Apocalypse of Peter* 81:4–24. Once again, there was a dialogue between Peter and Jesus, with Peter as the first speaker:

I saw him apparently being seized by them. And I said, "What am I seeing, O

Lord? Is it really you whom they take? And are you holding on to me? And are they hammering the feet and hands of another? Who is this one above the cross, who is glad and laughing?" The Savior said to me, "He whom you saw being glad and laughing above the cross is the Living Jesus. But he into whose hands and feet they are driving the nails is his fleshly part, which is the substitute. They put to shame that which remained in his likeness. And look at him, and [look at] me!"

This passage is a bit obscure, but the key point is that there were two beings: the living Lord and Savior Jesus, and the human substitute Jesus. The Savior was from the Father; He was a spiritual being who could have nothing essentially to do with flesh, bodies, or death. He could not be involved with a fallen and corrupt material existence. The earthly, living substitute, a mere human who only represented Jesus, was crucified. The heavenly Jesus did not suffer on the cross; His earthly substitute was sacrificed. The heavenly Jesus laughed at the world's ignorance.

A second text on Jesus comes from *Second Treatise of the Great Seth* 56:6–19. Seth was a son of Adam and Eve. This passage relates more teaching about Jesus and the cross, with Jesus speaking about His experience. It reads, "It was another . . . who drank the gall and the vinegar; it was not I. They struck me with the reed; it was another, Simon, who bore the cross on his shoulder. It was another upon whom they placed the crown of thorns. But I was rejoicing in the height . . . over their error . . . And I was laughing at their ignorance." This passage makes it clear that the one incarnate Son of God, Jesus Christ, did not suffer on the cross. Actually to think that the Jesus Christ of heaven was on the cross was an error. The view seems to be that the Savior from heaven, the spiritual Jesus, was too pure and transcendent to suffer on the cross. This *Seth* text and the *Apocalypse of Peter* say the same thing about Jesus.

The third text treating Jesus' resurrection presence comes from *Acts of John* 93, and John spoke about his experience of Jesus. This text reads, "I will tell you another glory, brothers, sometimes when I meant to touch him I encountered a material, solid body; but at other times again when I felt him, his substance was immaterial and incorporeal . . . as if it did not exist at all." Here we see the ambivalence over whether

Jesus had a real human body and presence. In the same passage John checked for footprints, but Jesus left none. Neither did Jesus blink. Jesus is a spiritual being. His humanity is a "phantom," one of surface appearance only, not real human substance. The Jesus from the heavenly Father is too transcendent to be human. The Incarnation is really an apparition. This "more divine" Jesus is the opposite of what *The Da Vinci Code* claims for these secret gospel texts; they do not have a more human Jesus but a more divine and removed Jesus. This is a different Jesus from the One to whom Mary Magdalene clung (John 20). That Jesus could be embraced. It is a different Jesus from the One who appeared to Thomas to show him the nail prints on His hands (John 20). That risen and exalted Jesus suffered on the cross.

The picture of a Jesus who lacked genuine humanity and did not know suffering is distinct from that of other Christians. For those who appealed to the apostolic preaching, it was one and the same Jesus who endured death (John 1:1–18; Rom. 3:21–26; 5:1–11; 1 John 1:1–4). He was the eternal Son of God, sent from the Father. That Son took on humanity. There is one, and only one, Jesus Christ, not a heavenly

Jesus and one who takes His place to suffer (Heb. 4:14–10:18). There is one who is Messiah, Son of God: incarnate, crucified, and raised (Acts 2:16–40; 1 Cor. 15:3–11). Titus 2:11–14 (NIV) puts it this way:

> For the grace of God that brings salvation has appeared to all men. It teaches us to say "No" to ungodliness and worldly passions, and to live self-controlled, upright and godly lives in this present age, while we wait for the blessed hope — the glorious appearing of our great God and Savior, Jesus Christ, who gave himself for us to redeem us from all wickedness and to purify for himself a people that are his very own, eager to do what is good.

Here is a Jesus, divine and divinely sent, who gives of Himself and suffers for us so we may have life.

Why does this difference matter? The Gnostic or Gnostic-like view means that there is no representation of Jesus on behalf of humanity. The issue of salvation is not a matter of dealing with sin or being a sacrifice on behalf of others. God does not deal with sin for us out of His goodness and grace. Nor does He really show that the depths of His love extend to His willingness to die so we can live. All of that vanishes in the view of these non–New Testament texts. Salvation resides in proper knowledge, grasping the mystery aright. In sum, salvation is up to us. This observation leads to another area of distinction, the matter of revelation and authority.

4. Revelation, Authority, and Spirituality in Defining the Faith

Another distinctive element in Gnostic or Gnostic-like views involves revelation, authority, and spirituality. *Apocalypse of Peter* 76:27–34 puts the issue this way: "Some who do not understand mystery speak of things they do not understand, but they will boast that the mystery of truth belongs to them alone." This text complains about the ignorant critics of the movement the *Apocalypse of Peter* represents. It is the critics who are ignorant and do not understand mystery. The *Testimony of Truth* 31:24–32:2 argues that those who criticize them claim to be Christian, but those very people do not know who Christ is. Elaine Pagels describes the conflict by writing, "Gnostic Christians . . . assert that what distinguishes the false from the true church is not its relationship to the clergy, but the level of understanding of its members, and the quality of their relationship to one another" (*The Gnostic Gospels*, p. 106).

Those who are enlightened are "from the life," as *Apocalypse of Peter* 70:20–71:5 puts it. That text reads:

He (Jesus) said to me, "Peter, blessed are those above belonging to the Father who revealed life to those who are from the life, through me, since I reminded [them], they who are built on what is strong, that they may hear my word and distinguish words of unrighteousness and transgression of law from righteousness, as being from the height of every word of this *pleroma* of truth, having been enlightened in good pleasure by him whom the principalities sought."

As we have seen in many of these texts, the issue is possession of secret knowledge, the *gnosis*. Jesus is merely a conduit to this higher knowledge. More important, no authority can challenge that revelation, which comes directly to a member of the group. The difference from more traditional Christians is that the role of the already extant, major texts of the faith is relativized and weakened. Also relativized is the impor-

110

tance of Jesus' unique work for humanity that dealt with the issue of sin from within.

The issue is not merely to know or understand the problem and have a proper, abstract conception of God, but to have been changed so that one can deal with the problem on the basis of having come into a meaningful relationship with God. Spirituality is about more than having right perception; it is about having a realistic perspective about God and oneself while being able to respond with openness to God and His leading.

The Gnostic believers in contemporary direct revelation complained about the authority of the bishops in the other Christian groups. The debate centered on who defined and spoke for the Christian faith. There was a distinct view of revelation and authority; Gnostics believed in a direct access to revelation that other Christian groups did not. Heracleon, a Gnostic commentator on John's gospel, in *Fragment* 13 as recorded by Origen in his *Commentary on John* 10.33, compared these other, non-Gnostic Christians to Levites shut out from mystery. This Gnostic group understood that the means to salvation was the knowledge brought to them by the heavenly Revealer-Savior, whom they associated

111

with the heavenly Supreme Father, the *Pleroma* of the upper world. That Father was different from the Father of this earthly, physical world with its *Demiurge*. Again, in contrast to the documents now found in the New Testament, this God was too great to be intimate with his followers. He might give light, but that light came through others. Contact with God was indirect. The light from God triggered a light within individuals that led to knowledge, with knowledge being the key to deliverance.

This self-understanding of one's origin, inner nature, and alliance to God led to freedom, ascent, and spiritual wealth. This inner, spiritual light led to spirituality and self-understanding. As Pagels notes, for this group "theology is really anthropology." In other words, exploring the psyche was a religious quest, the responsibility and work of the person seeking God (*The Gnostic Gospels*, p. 123). The major subject was the inner human being, not God. The major spiritual problem was *ignorance*, not sin. Ignorance of the mystery caused people to suffer. The *Gospel of Thomas* 45:30–33 said it like this: "If you bring forth what is within you, what you bring forth will save you. If you do not bring forth what is within you, what you do not bring forth will destroy you." The *Gospel of Thomas* 3 declared, "The kingdom is inside you, and outside you. When you come to know yourselves, then you will be known, and you will see that it is you who are the children of the living father. But if you will not know yourselves, you dwell in poverty, and it is you who are that poverty."

In this view, spirituality is not found by an association with the Jesus who walked the earth or a recognition of what His work says about who we are left to ourselves. Nor is spirituality driven by an alliance and allegiance to the living God in response to His love and care toward us. These themes of spirituality found in the New Testament are missing. Rather, spirituality merely means understanding who one is and seeking what God already has placed in each one of us.

On page 68 of her most recent work, *Beyond Belief: The Secret Gospel of Thomas*, Pagels discusses the messages of Thomas's gospel and John's gospel:

Now we can see how John's message contrasts with that of Thomas. Thomas's Jesus directs each disciple to discover the light within ("within a person of light there is light"); but John's Jesus declares instead that "I am the

113

light of the world" and that "whoever does not come to me walks in darkness." In Thomas, Jesus reveals to the disciples that "you are from the kingdom and to it you shall return" and teaches them to say for themselves that "we come from the light": but John's Jesus speaks as the only one who comes "from above" and so has rightful priority over everyone else: "You are from below; I am from above . . . The one who comes from above is above all."

Two distinct views of spirituality emerge, one rooted in Jesus (that of John's gospel) and one rooted in the divine potential in each one of us (Thomas's gospel). These are two different theologies, two different faiths.

5. A Lesser Issue: The Role of Women

The final difference, although of lesser importance if we examine how little their critics spoke about it, involved encouraging women to experience this revelation and be leaders in the community. Tertullian, a critic of the movement, complained loudly about the audacity of these women (*The Prescription Against Heretics* 41). He exclaimed, "The very women of these heretics, how wanton they are!" Tertullian was not in favor of women teaching, performing exorcisms, and baptizing. The claim of modern writers is that the openness toward women was a major point of contention between these Gnostics and their critics who had no room for female leaders. Remember, however, that we noted a Gnostic text, *Gospel of Thomas* 114, where females needed to become males to enter God's kingdom. When we read the early church critics of these Gnostics, we need to keep in mind that such complaints about gender were derivative complaints. The other issues — concerning secret revelation, God, Jesus, and authority independent of Jesus' work to deal with sin — most disturbed the ancient critics.

The Current Appeal to These Writings

A quick but representative survey of these works is important in appreciating what this material is and is not. Some suggest that Gnosticism shows how diverse Christianity was in the second century. In one sense, this is true. There was a significant enough group of people calling themselves Christians that other Christians wrote volumes to warn about their views. A survey of Gnostic beliefs, brief as it was, shows this sub-group's distinctive views of God, Jesus, salvation, revelation, and spirituality. How can one call such competing views part of the same faith? In fact, the vast difference between the two expressions of Christian faith led each faction to deny that the other faction was Christian. Each side was honest about its perception of the other because each side sensed how much was at stake in the competing views about God.

This *division* in the Christian house of the first three centuries must be noted in current treatments of Christianity, whether by novelists or some theologians. Those who appeal to these writings suggest that our understanding of the early Christian faith should be broad enough to encompass and appreciate both movements. We should not let the story of Christianity be dictated by the "winners" (what became known as orthodox Christianity). We should not exclude what the other Christian expressions (these Gnostic texts) can teach us.

For example, two quotations from Pagels's work *The Gnostic Gospels* reveal how such appeals are made. On page 69, she writes, "The Nag Hammadi sources, discovered at a time of contemporary social crises concerning sexual roles, challenge us to reinterpret history — and to re-evaluate the present situation." Later on page 150, in her conclusion after a helpful survey of these Gnostic texts, she states,

The concerns of gnostic Christians survived only as a suppressed current, like a river driven underground . . . Now that the Nag Hammadi discoveries give us a new perspective on this process, we can understand why certain creative persons throughout the ages from Valentinus and Heracleon to Blake, Rembrandt, Dostoevsky, Tolstoy, and Nietzsche, found themselves at the edges of orthodoxy . . . An increasing number of people today share their experience . . . All the old questions — the original questions, sharply debated at the beginning of Christianity — are being reopened: How is one to understand the resurrection? What about women's participation in priestly and episcopal office? Who was Christ, and how does he relate to the believer? What are the similarities between Christianity and other world religions?

She closes her book with this remark about the Nag Hammadi finds:

117

But they remained hidden until the twentieth century, when our cultural experience has given us a new perspective on the issues they raise. Today we read them with different eyes, not merely as "madness and blasphemy" but as Christians in the first centuries experienced them — a powerful alternative to what we know as orthodox Christian tradition. Only now are we beginning to consider the questions with which they confront us. (p. 151)

In her more recent book, *Beyond Belief*, Pagels makes another appeal. She discusses what she does not like about Christianity as a result of her study of the Nag Hammadi texts. On page 29, she states,

This research helped clarify what I cannot love: the tendency to identify Christianity with a single, authorized set of beliefs however these actually vary from church to church — coupled with the conviction that Christian belief alone offers access to God. Now that scholars have begun to place the sources discovered at Nag Hammadi, like newly discovered pieces of a complex puzzle, next to what we have long known from tradition, we find that these remarkable texts, only now becoming widely known, are transforming what we know about Christianity.

There is an agenda here. It is the rejection of Christian faith as a historically unified set of core beliefs held over the centuries starting from the earliest period. Pagels's appeal ignores early traditional Christianity and how in the church's emerging Scripture there was a core belief expressed in the ancient creeds that themselves reflected the most major and central points of the New Testament. This core is orthodoxy in the best sense of that term. It is a Christianity with very distinct emphases that differ from the Gnostic texts or the collection of "secret" gospels we have just surveyed.

Pagels's claims and appeals reflect an agenda whose goal is to revise that orthodox faith. That effort is rooted in these ancient so-called secret documents that historically operated on the fringe of Christianity.

Interestingly and ironically perhaps this view is asking for something that neither of the early Christian alternatives in its time would have accepted as a viable option. The lesson of history is that these two approaches to Christianity were so very different from each other as to be

119

incompatible from the view of each school.

Some variation among the four Gospels could be accepted within what we shall call traditional or orthodox Christianity (and these differences have been well documented for centuries). Yet there was never a persuasive combination that attempted to fuse all of these traditional expressions together with the more Gnostic-like ones in a manner that affirmed both views. So neither group could regard both expressions as Christian. One was claiming its roots in the past for understanding the faith in the apostolic testimony and tradition, while the other was claiming access now to a direct kind of revelation that was of more significance than past revelation. *This mutual acceptance that the other view was not Christian is something some modern historians in examining the movements seem unwilling to appreciate sufficiently.* It is a point worth remembering as some extol the secrets of this rediscovered variant of Christian faith.

Again, I will let the ancient writers speak for themselves. Writing at the turn of the third century, Tertullian reacted to the work of Marcion, who gave his own "scripture" to defend his ideas in the second century. In *Against Marcion*, book 4, chapter 4, Tertullian wrote,

We must follow, then, the clue of our discussion, meeting every effort of our opponents with reciprocal vigor. I say that *my* Gospel is the true one; Marcion, that *his* is. I affirm that Marcion's Gospel is adulterated; Marcion, that mine is. Now what is to settle the point for us, except it be that principle of *time,* which rules that the authority lies with that which shall be found to be more ancient; and assumes as an elemental truth, that corruption (of doctrine) belongs to the side which shall be convicted of comparative lateness in its origin. For, inasmuch as error is falsification of truth, it must needs be that truth therefore precedes error. A thing must exist prior to its suffering any casualty; and an object must precede all rivalry to itself. Else how absurd it would be, that, when we have proved our position to be the older one, and Marcion's the later, ours should yet appear to be the false one, before it had even received from truth its objective existence; and Marcion's should also be supposed to have experienced rivalry at our hands, even before its publication; and, in fine, that that should be thought to be the truer position which is the later one — a century later than the publication of all the many and great facts and records of the Christian religion, which certainly could not have been published *without,* that is to say, *before,* the truth of the gospel.

In the next chapter our investigation shall return to the age of the writings and the debate over what writings were seen as authoritative in selecting the gospels. However, there are two key points here: (1) each side in the ancient debate did not recognize the other as legitimate, and (2) the issue for those arguing for orthodoxy was the timing or age of the writings, as well as their content. In short, there was a real debate about real and substantive theological differences.

Why Does All of This Matter?

The recent increase in the number of popular books and articles spawned by this scholarship requires us to pay careful attention to what is happening in our popular culture. As I write, a new wave of popular, quasi nonfiction books is being released that is similar to *The Da Vinci Code.* It is almost a genre unto itself. The role of Mary Magdalene continues her meteoric rise in our culture. Yet the exaltation of Mary Magdalene and the morphing of her into a politically correct symbol have no solid root in early church history. One has to distort that history to give her that role. As seemingly pretty and appealing as virtual reality can be, it is not historical reality. Whatever the merits of the case being argued for the way that moderns should live, we cannot overlook that the appeal to ancient history for support is a distortion of that history.

In making a similar historical assessment as my own, Mathewes-Green points out the deficiencies of the new quest and the appeal for a new look at these other gospels:

Now you can begin to see what the early Christians found heretical. Gnosticism rejected the body and saw it as a prison for the soul; Christianity insisted that God infuses all creation and that even the human body can be a vessel of holiness, a "temple of the Holy Spirit." Gnosticism rejected the Hebrew Scriptures and portrayed the God of the Jews as an evil spirit; Christianity looked on Judaism as a mother. Gnosticism was élitist; Christianity was egalitarian, preferring "neither Jew nor Greek, male nor female, slave nor free." Finally, Gnosticism was just too complicated.

Christianity maintained the simple invitation of the One who said, "Let the little children come unto me." Full-blown science-fiction Gnosticism died under its own weight.

Pagels does not endorse this aspect of Gnosticism. But the Gnostics would not endorse her version either. They did not think of these elaborate schemes as mythopoeic (which is how Neo-Gnostics describe them), but as factual. Your salvation depended on getting it right, and Gnostics argued with each other much as theologians do today. Some claimed that the body was so evil you had to give up sex; others said the body was so illusory that it didn't matter what you did with it. A well-meaning postmodernist who murmured "You're both right" would be reviled for not grasping what's at stake.

Pagels's book *Beyond Belief* offers a selective look at this other kind of Christian faith through one slice of that movement, *The Gospel of Thomas*. The Mathewes-Green article cited here is a review of Pagels's latest book. This recent work, also climbing to unusual bestseller heights for a book on religion, is a prominent example of this call to reassess what we know about Christianity. Mathewes-Green describes and assesses the plot line of *Beyond Belief*:

This best-selling book, and its accompanying train of reviews and author profiles, presents a familiar cast of characters. The Gnostics, developers of a variety of Christ-flavored spiritualities in the earliest centuries of the Christian era, are enthroned as noble seekers of enlightenment. The early Church, which rejected these theologies, is assigned its usual role of oppressor, afflicting believers with rigid Creeds. It's the old story of oppressive bad guys and rebellious good guys, and Americans never tire of it.

But a look at the supposedly scandalous material comes up short. The most-cited Gnostic text, the Gospel of Thomas, mixes familiar sayings of Jesus with others of more mystical bent. These are sometimes cryptic but hardly outrageous. They're not far different from Christian poetry and mysticism through the ages. Where's the problem?

Well, not here. Early Christians rejected Gnosticism, all right. But what Pagels presents is not the part they rejected.

125

What they rejected, Pagels does not present.

Mathewes-Green says in short form what this chapter has tried to show — that a full consideration of these texts reveals a theology very distinct from the faith in the biblical materials. We cannot be selective in what to highlight from this material. There was a theological package on offer in this material, and we should be aware of all their components. Picking and choosing snippets from this material and quickly passing over the rest of the package leave an imbalance in what was being affirmed by this ancient movement. Modern writings affirming the value of this material are picking and choosing for the most part; they are not giving us the full story. The goal in investigating this code has been to fill in the gaps so that we have the full picture.

There is one final point. Our critical investigation of this new, attention-getting scholarship and the popular works it is spawning is not criticism from the fringe. I could point to the fine study by the historian Philip Jenkins, *Hidden Gospels: How the Search for Jesus Lost Its Way* (2001). He documented that among other academics like me, there is an awareness of this recasting of history. On page 208, he stated, "Much modern writing on the hidden gospels and their authors are utterly partisan, with well-defined heroes and villains who are represented quite as starkly and stereotypically as the white-robed saints of motion picture notoriety." On page 216, he concluded:

Diligent exploration of the very large literature of New Testament scholarship over the last century or so might suggest that the "new" insight is nothing of the kind, however conveniently the work of past generations will be overlooked. As we have seen, a kind of historical amnesia is a necessary feature of the whole myth of concealment and discovery.

This *new* scholarship of historical revisionism is a cause worth noting. *Here we begin to discover the real secret and code behind* The Da Vinci Code. *It is nothing less than a conscious effort to obscure the uniqueness and vitality of the Christian faith and message.* Historians as well as members of the Catholic, Orthodox, and Protestant faiths are raising significant questions about this "new way's" historical credibility. Readers of such works should be in the know about what is going on and why it matters. Such

127

gnosis should not be a secret; the public has a right to know.

What Can We Say About the Secret Gospels?

Our investigation has moved rather quickly through the fascinating and distinctive material that makes up the so-called secret gospels. In many ways, this material contains a religious code all its own. We have seen that the secret is not so much about this material's recent rediscovery and investigation. Rather, *secret* is a term that highlights the internal emphasis of these ancient texts. For this wing of ancient Christian expression, to know the secrets is to experience knowledge and salvation. This knowledge involved views of God very distinct from the views that have driven the major wings of the traditional church. Each side in this dispute recognized that the other side represented a very distinct expression of Christianity. One could not easily be both a Gnostic and a tradition-based Christian. One view was too directly revelatory for the other, not to mention the very different views of the Creator God, Jesus, the cross, and salvation. Although some wish to make gender a major issue in these differences, that topic was a minor source of irritation between the views in comparison to the other key theological differences.

Given these differences, it is inevitable that in the subsequent centuries of the early church, a sorting out of views emerged. Code 4 has been broken. What is represented in the secret gospels and related texts is an expression of Christianity vastly different from that in the texts with which we are familiar in the New Testament. Neither side in this dispute sought a coming together. Even as the tradition-based Christians complained about error and heresy, so did the Gnostics. The Gnostics referred to the leaders of the competitive view as "empty channels" (*Apocalypse of Peter* 79:30). In *Testimony of Truth* 34:26, it was said of the traditionalists, "They do not have the Word which gives [life]."

This dispute between Gnostics and traditionally rooted Christians was not a matter of trying to gain entrance into and share the faith; it was about who represented the faith. To suggest otherwise is to participate in a form of revisionism that does not appreciate the original setting or nature of the differences we have just investigated. The impression that Christians shared a vast array of writings that some reduced in number to produce Scripture of their own later design ignores this debate's contentious nature from early on. This dispute erupted from the moment these two expressions of faith emerged. Once again an element of *The Da Vinci Code* is exposed and shown to be less than "fact."

So what about the writings that are more familiar to us, namely, the four Gospels? Why did some texts receive more prominent status? What process led to their emergence as central to the faith of so many Christians? We turn now to Code 5.

Code 5

HOW WERE THE NEW TESTAMENT GOSPELS ASSEMBLED?

In yet another foray into history, Teabing makes a series of assertions about the development of Christianity on pages 231–35 of *The Da Vinci Code*. If the discussion about the Gnostic gospels is the most problematic of this character's claims, then his treatment of Constantine and Nicea is a close second. Here Teabing argues that Constantine "commissioned and financed a new Bible, which omitted those gospels that spoke of Christ's *human* traits and embellished those gospels that made Him godlike. The earlier gospels were outlawed, gathered up, and burned" (p. 234). It is in this context that Teabing notes the finds at Nag Hammadi, a major source for the texts we just examined in Code 4. The Vatican is made responsible for suppressing the release of these texts. The modern Bible "was compiled and edited by men who possessed a political agenda — to promote the divinity of the man Jesus Christ and use His influence to solidify

131

their own power base."

At least here another character, Langdon, makes a reply about sincerity of belief before Teabing claims that "almost everything our fathers taught us about Christ is *false*" (emphasis in *The Da Vinci Code*, p. 235). Constantine and the Council of Nicea in A.D. 325 are held culpable for collating the Bible and voting for Jesus' divinity when "until *that* moment in history, Jesus was viewed by His followers as a mortal prophet" (emphasis in *The Da Vinci Code*, p. 233). Again Teabing, the novel's "theologian," speaks, "Christ as Messiah was critical to the functioning of Church and state. Many scholars claim that the early Church literally *stole* Jesus from His original followers, hijacking His human message, shrouding it in an impenetrable cloak of divinity, and using it to expand their own power." It was by a "relatively close vote" at that council that Jesus was made Son of God.

In doing so, Teabing goes on to explain, "Because Constantine upgraded Jesus' status four centuries *after* Jesus' death, thousands of documents already existed chronicling His [Jesus'] life as a *mortal* man. To rewrite the history books, Constantine knew he would need a bold stroke. From

132

this sprang the most profound moment in Christian history" (emphasis in *The Da Vinci Code*, p. 234). In other words, Constantine and the council ignored a whole swath of documents in giving Jesus a greater status than He previously had possessed. The claim is that Christianity, as we now know it, is really a creation of the fourth century, not the first. However, note the appeal Teabing makes to scholars who argue that Jesus' human message was hijacked and turned into something that made Jesus into a God by the later church. Here is where the novel and scholarship converge. *The Da Vinci Code* is appealing to the "Scholars' Code."

In these claims, two ideas are brought together, both of which need examination. They are the manner in which the New Testament Gospels emerged as central to Christian belief and the issue of Jesus' divinity. We tackle the topics in the reverse order. The issues that need investigation here are (1) what Christians believed and when they began believing it, and (2) what took place before Nicea was held. In other words, before Nicea, what did Christians believe, and where can we find evidence of what they believed?

Before we examine these questions, we

133

need to note three points in *The Da Vinci Code* that have some validity. First, there is no doubt that Constantine was a key figure and that his rule was a turning point in Christian history. In the centuries leading up to Constantine's power, Christians had suffered persecution and martyrdom; all of that changed when the emperor gave his support to Christianity. Second, the Nicene Creed was an important affirmation in the history of the faith and was, in part, an effort to control what was to be believed. The creed was an attempt to affirm the core of what Christians regarded as essential for all Christians to believe, a significant exercise for a movement experiencing the diversity that Christianity faced in A.D. 325. Third, the collection of texts into an official list that became the canon of Scripture gained momentum in this period. A result of that process was that documents on the other side of this dispute were destroyed, and their influence waned.

This council and the creed represented what a sizable number of Christian communities had believed for more than two hundred years. That was a major reason this view found support at this council. The Nicene Creed put in precise philosophical and theological language what had been expressed in more general terms for years. It also affirmed which texts taught such views. What is more, the four Gospels highlighted at this council had been solidly established and recognized in these communities for more than a century before Nicea. The vote at Nicea, rather than establishing the church's beliefs, affirmed and officially recognized what was already the church's dominant view. The canon and how we got it is a story that starts with beliefs about Jesus.

The Divinity of Jesus: By Vote or by Conviction?

So what did the Christians believe? When did they believe it? Was the adoption of Jesus' divinity a fourth-century political move? For the record, the Nicene Creed of A.D. 325 reads as follows:

We believe in one God, the Father All-sovereign, maker of heaven and earth, and of all things visible and invisible; And in one Lord Jesus Christ, and the only-begotten Son of God, Begotten of the Father before all the ages, Light of Light, true God of true God, begotten not made, of one substance with the Father, through whom all things were made; who for us men and for our salvation came down from the heavens, and was made flesh of the Holy Spirit and the Virgin Mary, and became man, and was crucified for us under Pontius Pilate, and suffered and was buried, and rose again on the third day according to the Scriptures, and ascended into the heavens, and sits on the right hand of the Father, and comes again with glory to judge living and dead, of whose kingdom there shall be no end:

And in the Holy Spirit, the Lord and the Life-giver, that proceeds from the Father, who with the Father and Son is worshipped together and glorified together, who spoke through the prophets:

In one holy catholic and apostolic church:

We acknowledge one baptism unto remission of sins. We look for a resurrection of the dead, and the life of the age to come.

1. The First-Century Evidence from Paul and Early Traditional Materials

Our investigative search takes us not only to the Gospels but also to the apostle Paul, a Jew who in his own words had persecuted Christians and approved of their arrest and execution until he saw the risen Jesus (Gal. 1:11–24). This event produced a personal revolution in his theological view. The writings from Paul date between A.D. 50 and 68, almost three hundred years before Nicea. Paul used traditional materials showing that others shared and confessed his core theological beliefs. No one knew who Constantine was when Paul wrote. Two key classes of texts permit us to see Paul's theology and the theology of others who shared his views: those that involve a confessional statement of the church, and places where he referred to Jesus using language from the Old Testament that pertained to God.

The first class of texts involves confessional statements like 1 Corinthians 8:5–6 (RSV). Paul noted that while those in the world around him worshiped many gods, he and the Christians worshiped one God and one Lord Jesus Christ: "Although there may be so-called gods in heaven or on earth — as indeed there are many 'gods' and many 'lords' — yet for us there is one God, the Father, from whom are all things and for whom we exist, and one Lord, Jesus Christ, through whom are all things and through whom we exist."

The title "Lord" often referred to God. In the Greek Bible of the Jews, a work known as the Septuagint, the title "Lord" often substituted for "God." To call Jesus Christ Lord was to refer to His deity, especially in a passage that mentioned other gods of the religious faith of others. According to Paul, Jesus was involved in the Creation as Creator. For a person of Jewish background, that would be the declaration of an activity of God the Creator. Centuries before Nicea, a major Christian leader was affirming the divinity of Jesus not by the mere use of a title, but by a description of activity.

A second class of texts in Paul involves substitution texts like Philippians 2:9–11 (RSV). Without embarrassment, Paul applied to Jesus language that the prophet Isaiah applied to God in the Hebrew Bible. This text reads, "God has highly exalted him and bestowed on him the name which is above every name, that at the name of Jesus every knee should bow, in heaven and on earth and under the earth, and every tongue confess that Jesus Christ is Lord, to the glory of God the Father." In this passage, Jesus is the object of worship as every knee bows before Him, even as He bears the title of Lord. The language comes from Isaiah 45:23 where the prophet cited God as speaking ("By myself I have sworn, from my mouth has gone forth in righteousness a word that shall not return: 'To me every knee shall bow, every tongue shall swear' " [RSV]). Jesus is placed in the same position as God. Jesus receives homage as God does. These are not the only texts where this occurs in Paul. And it occurs in other writings from other authors of what became the New Testament (for example, Ps. 102:25–27 in Heb. 1:1–13). Jesus is not a mere prophet in these texts. He shares equal glory and honor with God.

2. The First-Century Evidence from the Rest of the New Testament

Paul was not alone. The gospel of John, probably written in the nineties of the first century, contains an unambiguous statement of Jesus' divinity in its first chapter (RSV):

In the beginning was the Word, and the Word was with God, and all that God was, the Word was [NET; alternatively, and the Word was God, RSV]. (v. 1)

He was in the beginning with God; all things were made through him. (vv. 2–3)

And the Word became flesh. (v. 14)

John made it clear in this opening to his gospel that the Word became flesh is Jesus, the actual and full incarnation of deity. Once again, participation in the Creation pointed to deity, just as Paul argued.

Some suggest that what Paul and John affirmed about Jesus stands in contrast to the other three gospels. This would be misleading. Mark, Matthew, and Luke were written, probably in this order, sometime between the sixties and eighties. These dates are debated among scholars, and I use the least conservative range. These are also first-century documents, and they tell the story of Jesus in a more restrained manner than is found in John, by which I mean they are less overt in attributing deity to Jesus. They tell Jesus' story "from the earth up." I document this point in my study of Jesus called *Jesus According to Scripture*, where I examine every passage on Jesus in Matthew through John. In other words, the first three gospels tell the story like a narrative or even a mystery working up to their final confession of who Jesus is. But make no mistake, all three ultimately declare Jesus to be God.

In these gospels, when Jesus is taken to be crucified, He is put to death for being blasphemous. Jesus claimed that God would indicate that Jesus was Son of man, One who was seated at the right hand of God and rode the clouds (something only deity does in the Bible). This is the same divine honor and glory shared with God that Paul and John referred to in their writings. All of these writings agree that Jesus is divine.

In the background of this Son of man statement were two ideas, both of which suggested a unique status for Jesus. One was the imagery of the Son of man, a human figure in Daniel 7:9–13 who will be given divine authority to judge at the end and will be brought into God's presence. The other was that this figure will sit with God in heaven, not just visit God in heaven. These ideas pointed to a unique vindication of Jesus. The Jews who heard this utterance believed that Jesus blasphemed, which meant He insulted the unique dignity of God by His claim. To understand the Jewish background of the scene is to appreciate the exalted self-claim that Jesus was making.

The details of this view of Jesus and its background are treated in a full study of two hundred pages I wrote years ago while doing research at the University of Tübingen in Germany. In *Blasphemy and Exaltation in Judaism and the Final Examination of Jesus* I consider the Jewish view of who gets to sit with God in heaven and under what circumstances. At the examination before the Jewish leaders Jesus' claims were either a unique and legitimate exaltation or remarks that offended the unique glory of God.

The Gospels recorded the event to make clear their view. In light of Jesus' subsequent resurrection, Jesus is a divine figure worthy to sit in God's presence because He is capable of sharing God's unique glory. We shall come back to this later. For now, understand that these Gospels and Paul's writings, first-century documents, portrayed Jesus as a fully human figure and as One who uniquely bears the full marks and honor of deity. These beliefs were widespread in Christianity almost three full centuries before Nicea.

I am not alone in holding this view and in arguing for it in detail. Larry Hurtado, professor of New Testament at the University of Edinburgh, has produced a recent study that traces the history of this understanding of Jesus through the early centuries, even beyond the period of the earliest texts. It reinforces what is argued here. His book, *Lord Jesus Christ: Devotion to Jesus in Earliest Christianity* (2003), raises questions about aspects of this "new" reading of the history that argues Jesus was not believed to be divine until the fourth century.

3. What Can We Say About the Age of the View That Jesus Was Divine?

Again, *The Da Vinci Code* is broken and found wanting. The idea that Jesus was divine did not result from a vote three hundred years after the time of Jesus. To suggest that the view of Jesus' divinity came so late, as Teabing does in the novel (p. 233), is to advance pure fiction and bad history. The view has clear expression in the books written within generations of the time of Jesus and has its roots in His closest followers.

But what of the assembling of these books that became a part of the New Testament? How did these books become a part of what theologians call the *canon,* a term that simply means a "standard"? Did a vote at Nicea make them so and exclude other books?

What About the Canon and the Making of the New Testament?

The naming of the books of the New Testament is part of a long process that extended from the writing of the documents in the latter half of the first century until they were fully recognized in the middle of the fourth century. In his book *The Canon of the New Testament*, Princeton New Testament scholar Bruce Metzger details the story given an overview here. In A.D. 367, Athanasius was the first to list the twenty-seven books of the New Testament as they exist in most Christian circles today. He also was the first to use the term *canon* for this collection. This list actually comes after Nicea (A.D. 325). Yet the history of this collection process shows that by the end of the second century, the four Gospels had, because of their roots, content, and usage, surfaced as the primary sources of Jesus' life and ministry.

Four forces drove the effort to define which gospel documents bore unique authority for Christians. They were apostolic roots as a ground for truth, widespread use (known as catholicity), the rise of competing views of the faith, and persecution. I combine the discussion of the first three forces; the apostolic roots and recognition of the authority of these works led to their widespread use, while the emergence of works with competing views led to the solidification of which works were deemed authoritative.

1. The Fourfold Gospel: Apostolic Roots As a Ground for Truth, Widespread Use, and the Threat of False Teaching

In all of the citations here from second- and third-century documents, the already preeminent position of the four Gospels is affirmed. This affirmation comes alongside the recognition that the existence of competing views of the faith made their relevance even more important. The fourfold gospel appeals to apostolic roots and truth to deal with the issue of false teaching.

The works of second-century theologians like Irenaeus and third-century theologians like Tertullian make it clear that the existence of groups like the Ebionites (a legalistic second-century group) and others led by Marcion (active by 140), Montanus (active by 170), and Valentinus (ca. 100–175) produced pressure to identify not only the core theological beliefs of Christians, but also the key documents.

In addition, lists of received books by the church date from this period. These lists noted which books were accepted by the churches and were read in services. In the centuries before the printing press, most Christians came to know these books not by having their own Bibles but by hearing these books read in church services. One of the most important of those lists is a Latin work known as the *Muratorian Canon*. It was discovered in 1740 by the Italian historian Ludovico Antonio Muratori, and so it bears his name. It is eighty-five lines long and broken off at the start, one of those famous gaps in an ancient text. The manuscript, which is a copy of the original document, appears to be from the eighth century. The document's reference to the fact that the *Shepherd of Hermes* was recently written and that Pius I had recently been bishop (d. 157) tells us that the original list probably goes back to the late second century, or 150 years before Nicea, although the point about dating is debated with some pushing its date back to the fourth century.

Following the broken part, the document states, "The third book of the gospel is that according to Luke." It names only four Gospels as containing "the gospel." In fact, it refers to John this way: "The fourth of the gospels is that of John, one of the disciples." Here we have second-century evidence that "the gospel" was contained in the four Gospels and in them alone. This list is interesting as well because later it notes that the church receives only the apocalypses of John and Peter, though Peter's apocalypse is questioned by some as suitable for reading in the church. The *Muratorian Canon* explicitly names works by Valentinus and Marcion that are to be excluded from the church.

Second-century church father Irenaeus wrote *Against Heresies*, in which he defended and explained the faith rooted in the tradition that had been passed on. In Book 3.11.7 he clarified the core of the faith and the groups against whom he was writing in his works. This text reads:

7. Such, then, are the first principles of the Gospel: that there is one God, the Maker of this universe; He who was also announced by the prophets, and who by Moses set forth the dispensation of the law, — [principles] which proclaim the Father of our Lord Jesus Christ, and ignore any other God or Father except Him. So firm is the ground upon which these Gospels rest, that the very heretics themselves bear witness to them, and, starting from these [documents], each one of them endeavors to establish his own peculiar doctrine. For the Ebionites, who use Matthew's Gospel only, are confuted out of this very same, making false suppositions with regard to the Lord. But Marcion, mutilating that

according to Luke, is proved to be a blasphemer of the only existing God, from those [passages] which he still retains. Those, again, who separate Jesus from Christ, alleging that Christ remained impassible, but that it was Jesus who suffered, preferring the Gospel by Mark, if they read it with a love of truth, may have their errors rectified. Those, moreover, who follow Valentinus, making copious use of that according to John, to illustrate their conjunctions, shall be proved to be totally in error by means of this very Gospel, as I have shown in the first book. Since, then, our opponents do bear testimony to us, and make use of these [documents], our proof derived from them is firm and true.

Irenaeus made several points. First, he noted the ground of his faith was what the key Gospels affirmed, not just portions of them. He criticized the Ebionites because they used only Matthew, Marcion because he used only selected portions of Luke, and Valentinus because he used John's gospel selectively. Irenaeus was not selecting documents for use; he was affirming that four Gospels — Matthew, Mark, Luke, and John — in their entirety reflected the core testimony about Jesus. Second, Irenaeus reacted to opposing views of Christianity, accusing others of developing "peculiar doctrine," which, among other errors, separated Jesus from the Christ in terms of Jesus' suffering. These views were somewhat like those described in our examination of the Gnostic gospels. As stated in the last chapter, we see clear evidence of opposing views of Christianity as well as which gospels, and what parts of these gospels, best represented Christianity.

In the next chapter, 3.11.8, of *Against Heresies*, Iranaeus explained why there could be only four key Gospels. He expressed his conviction of the preeminence of the four Gospels when he wrote:

8. It is not possible that the Gospels can be either more or fewer in number than they are. For, since there are four zones of the world in which we live, and four principal winds, while the Church is scattered throughout all the world, and the "pillar and ground" of the Church is the Gospel and the spirit of life; it is fitting that she should have four pillars, breathing out immortality on every side, and vivifying men afresh. From which fact, it is evident that the Word, the Arti-

ficer of all, He that sits upon the cherubim, and contains all things, He who was manifested to men, has given us the Gospel under four aspects, but bound together by one Spirit. As also David says, when entreating His manifestation, "Thou that sits between the cherubim, shine forth." For the cherubim, too, were four-faced, and their faces were images of the dispensation of the Son of God.

Later in the same passage, Irenaeus coined an expression that summarized well the view of the church in this period, "the gospel is quadriform," or the one gospel is expressed in the four Gospels:

Such, then, as was the course followed by the Son of God, so was also the form of the living creatures; and such as was the form of the living creatures, so was also the character of the Gospel. For the living creatures are quadriform, and the Gospel is quadriform (four-fold), as is also the course followed by the Lord. For this reason were four principal covenants given to the human race: one, prior to the deluge, under Adam; the second, that after the deluge, under

Noah; the third, the giving of the law, under Moses; the fourth, that which renovates man, and sums up all things in itself by means of the Gospel, raising and bearing men upon heavenly kingdom.

Irenaeus was not creating a fourfold gospel; he was presenting reasons he found compelling to accept its existence. In other words, the fourfold gospel already existed. The fourfold gospel contained the gospel. The four works stood at the core of faith for Christians who sought roots in the teaching of the apostles and those who heard them.

For Irenaeus, apostolic roots supported the validity of the Gospels. In *Against Heresies* 3.1.1 he explained it this way:

We have learned from none others the plan of our salvation, than from those through whom the Gospel has come down to us, which they did at one time proclaim in public, and, at a later period, by the will of God, handed down to us in the Scriptures, to be the ground and pillar of our faith. For it is unlawful to assert that they preached before they possessed "perfect knowledge," as some do even venture to say, boasting themselves as improvers of the apostles. For,

151

after our Lord rose from the dead, [the apostles] were invested with power from on high when the Holy Spirit came down [upon them], were filled from all [His gifts], and had perfect knowledge: they departed to the ends of the earth, preaching the glad tidings of the good things [sent] from God to us, and proclaiming the peace of heaven to men, who indeed do all equally and individually possess the Gospel of God.

In this text, Irenaeus criticized those who thought they could improve on the apostles. This text reveals that the debate between the groups was over revelation and authority, a fact we noted in the discussion of the Gnostic gospels and the views associated with such works. Irenaeus rejected the idea that "perfect knowledge" (remember their emphasis on *gnosis*) came after these core gospel texts. The debate surrounding these Gospels was whether they were so rooted in apostolic connection that they were fully adequate to communicate the faith or whether more revelation was required. For Irenaeus, the answer was that these Gospels were adequate. No further revelation was necessary.

When I speak of apostolic connection, I

mean not that these four Gospels were written by apostles, but that the Gospels were in contact with them. Nothing makes this more evident than the inclusion of Mark and Luke among the four, neither of whom was a member of the twelve apostles. What was believed and asserted was that Mark had contact with Peter, and Luke had contact with Paul, by now considered to have authority like the Twelve, as well as with others among the twelve apostles.

Irenaeus believed John and Matthew were the authors of these Gospels, something that is debated among New Testament scholars today, although most accept that these Gospels were rooted in groups that had contact with these apostles. Others today defend Irenaeus's views about the apostolic authorship of Matthew and John. The key point here, despite modern debate over authorship, is that these texts have an inherent claim to apostolic roots that the other gospels lacked. That is one reason why they circulated so widely. That is also why Irenaeus's opponents regarded them as sources that had to be used in making their case. In the view of these Fathers, the apostolic roots were associated with the guarantee that these texts taught the faith accurately. As Irenaeus suggested, one cannot improve upon the apostles.

Justin Martyr, writing even earlier in the second century than Irenaeus, referred to the gospels as "the memoirs which I say were drawn up by His apostles and those who followed them" (*Dialogue with Trypho* 103.19). He used the phrase "memoirs of the apostles" fifteen times in this work. The plural use of the term *memoirs* makes it clear there was more than one gospel in this grouping of texts. These references cite Matthew, Mark, and Luke. In *Dialogue* 106.3 Justin Martyr referred to the gospel of Mark as the "memoir of Peter" in line with the traditional association of Mark with Peter. His *I Apology* 66.3 referred to the "memoirs of the apostles" and then noted they were also called "gospels," suggesting the title was well known then for the writings. He also mentioned the written gospel in *Dialogue* 10.2 and 100.1.

These and other writers saw the value of these gospel texts and defended them on the basis of their roots in the apostles. These were the recollections of individuals who had walked with Jesus. The belief that the *Gospel of Thomas* and the other later gospels lacked such genuine apostolic connection caused many Christians not to accept them as reflective of the faith in its earliest form.

Tatian, a second-century student of Justin Martyr, became a follower of Valentinus, for which he was expelled from the Roman community to which he belonged. He combined the four Gospels into one account around A.D. 172. It was called the *Diatessaron*, which is Greek for "through the four." It was the first attempt to harmonize the Gospels into one continuous story of Jesus; the large bulk of this work is the four Gospels with a few other sources added. Even those on the side of the Gnostics recognized the centrality of these Gospels by the end of the second century. Moreover, the church never accepted Tatian's work as a replacement for the four Gospels, even though such a move could have made sense by simplifying the presentation of Jesus into one story. The four Gospels were too important and too well established to be combined into one account.

Later we come to Origen (185–254). In his first homily on Luke 1:1, according to the Latin translation of Jerome, Origen stated:

I know a certain gospel which is called "The Gospel according to Thomas" and a "Gospel according to Matthias," and

155

many others have we read — lest we should in any way be considered ignorant because of those who imagine they possess some knowledge if they are acquainted with these. Nevertheless, among all these we have approved solely what the church has recognized, which is that only the four gospels should be accepted.

This understanding is confirmed in a citation from Origen in the *Ecclesiastical History* of Eusebius from the fourth century. Origen, in his *Commentary of the Gospel of Matthew*, defended the idea of a recognized set of books for the church: "Among the four gospels, which are the only indisputable ones in the Church of God under heaven, I have learned by tradition that first was written that according to Matthew." He then explained that Mark was second; Luke, third; and after them all, John. These citations came from a figure who lived one hundred years before Nicea, and they echoed what we heard from other early, ancient writers. Most of the church recognized only four Gospels. The others were explicitly excluded.

I have said that apostolic roots, widespread usage, and the pressure of alternative expressions of Christianity led to the identification of those documents that were deemed most reflective of the earliest faith. Every text cited here was written more than a century before Constantine and Nicea. In fact, the need to name some books, both Gospels and Epistles, as canonical arose in part because some of those on the other side of the debate, such as Montanus in the second century, began to name books they wanted to promote as authoritative in contrast to what others were using. The debate over which books spoke for the faith was a debate over revelation and authority, with each side making distinctive claims.

Irenaeus's full list had twenty-one books, including all four Gospels. The four Gospels and much of the Pauline collection were the earliest part of what later became known as the New Testament. These Gospels and the bulk of the Pauline collection were already well established and circulated by A.D. 200. Discussion about the canon after that time involved approximately a dozen other books before the final number of twenty-seven emerged in the fourth century. Some made the final cut; others did not. But the gospels of Matthew, Mark, Luke, and John were there from the beginning of the process, and that is the point to remember in light of the claim of *The Da Vinci Code* that such Gospels were made into authorities later on.

2. Persecution

Another factor predating Constantine that contributed to the naming of such books was persecution. In some persecutions of the second to early fourth centuries the sacred books of the Christians were ordered to be burned or destroyed. The decree came from Emperor Diocletian in A.D. 303. To follow the order and destroy those books, authorities had to identify them and be able to name them. Those who would defy such an order needed to know which books were worth dying for.

So four factors drove the desire to name the central books of the faith: apostolic roots, widespread usage, the pressure of alternative expressions of Christianity, and persecution. The claim to be rooted in the apostles' witness and the extensive usage as a result dominated the acceptance process for the four Gospels. The books were not so much selected as recognized for their importance to the church. Their roots were seen as a guarantee of their veracity. Every cited text in this chapter predated Constantine by more than a century. In fact, by the time of Constantine, the four Gospels were already ancient.

What Can We Say About the Four Gospels As a Part of the Canon?

The recognition of the four Gospels as important sources for Christians significantly predates Constantine and the Council of Nicea. Their use, even by those whom the traditionally based Christians opposed, shows that they were well established as sources. Based on a reading of the writings of the earliest church, Matthew and John were the most popular and widely cited of the four Gospels, with Luke and Mark next in usage. Mark tended to be the least cited because most of his content was paralleled in Matthew and Luke.

There is another subtle point to our argument. We have not asked whether these secret gospels make claims that are historically true. Do they go back to Jesus? Do they reflect His teaching? Do their emphases reflect what He emphasized? Or are they rubbish? One could raise these questions and find these texts wanting. Our argument has not gone there, except to raise the questions by the claims that the gospels are more removed as a group from the apostolic period than their competitors. My point is more subtle. Even if we take these texts and their teaching at face value, they do not support what the "new" school supporting the value of the Gnostic gospels claims for them. These texts, on each side of the debate, force a choice. Either the Gnostic texts reflect what Jesus was and is, or the four Gospels are the best witnesses to the movement that Jesus generated. One cannot have it both ways.

A widely recognized Roman Catholic New Testament scholar, Raymond Brown, reviewed the book *The Gnostic Gospels* for the *New York Times* in November 1979. He commented that what these second- and third-century Christians did in moving to recognize these books and in rejecting others was to reject "only the rubbish of the second century," and he added, "It is still rubbish."

Code 5 is broken. Attributing the selection of the Gospels to Constantine and the Council of Nicea ignores more than a century of widespread use and recognition of these four Gospels. There was never a time when most church leaders were picking and choosing from dozens of gospels. To suggest otherwise is to morph Constantine into a figure he never was. The four Gospels were well established long before Constantine was born.

Having examined why certain texts were accepted and others were not, we now can return to the role of Mary Magdalene and others in the early church. The most difficult parts of our investigation are completed. We have seen that much of what *The Da Vinci Code* sets forth as fact really is not. The issues the book raises about gender in the early church still need attention. We turn to it next in Code 6.

Code 6

DOES MARY'S HONORED ROLE AS APOSTLE MATCH THE CLAIMS OF THE NEW SCHOOL?

As I write, a cover story in *Newsweek* titled "The Bible's Lost Stories" has just hit the newsstands. It is a discussion of the role of women in the church — and in the early church. The key players are scholars at prestigious schools including Harvard and Princeton working with the portrayal of Mary Magdalene in many of the texts we have been discussing. The *Gospel of Mary* and other such texts serve as best supporting actors in this article. The piece fits well with something else we see in *The Da Vinci Code*. The novel claims a special leadership role in the church for Mary Magdalene that later was suppressed. Alongside the theory that Jesus was married to her, there also was the claim that she "singlehandedly could crumble the Church" (p. 243). The church defamed Mary, because of her familial and leadership roles, and turned her into a prostitute to limit the influence of women and to

162

deny women the leadership role in the church Jesus had given them.

It is here as well that the novel introduces its theory that Mary is present in Leonardo da Vinci's *The Last Supper*. There also is the idea that the Holy Grail is Mary, reflecting her stealth role as part of Jesus' bloodline. The novel claims that the Da Vinci masterpiece exhibits a V-shaped layout to the left of Jesus as one looks at the painting. This V is the symbol of the feminine and tells us that Mary is in the painting as a leader in the church (p. 238; this remark does not tell you that the right side of the painting has another slightly less prominent V shape, but no one argues there are two women in the painting). So Mary was told to establish the church. Jesus was "the original feminist" (p. 248). This female role was such a threat to the predominantly male church that they made women the enemy and used their full political clout to defame Mary's reputation, turning her into a prostitute (p. 244).

Now, this claim is complex. It is one of the few places in the novel where there is some merit to certain aspects of what is affirmed. The claim is exaggerated, however. The "suppression of Mary" theory is overdrawn. All the relevant, ancient evidence needs a fresh look.

The suppression claim has the support of some scholars working in the area of these newly brought-to-the-surface Christian writings. The whole discussion is an example of what happens when we lack much evidence for something and efforts are made to fill in the blanks; virtually anything can go in the blanks and appear plausible.

In a sense here the claim about Christianity is: "In the beginning, there was the full, new, early story of the Christian faith, one suppressed by the church for centuries." At its root is a desire by some modern scholars to revise our understanding of the church and its history, a point we noted in discussing these new, so-called secret gospels.

Presenting this idea in the words of some who argue for it seems the best way to proceed. We start with a professor from Harvard. In Karen King's *The Gospel of Mary of Magdala: Jesus and the First Woman Apostle*, the author presents what she calls the "master story" of Christianity. A "master story" controls history or gives a defining historical view of a given topic. Here the master story is the one told by the church fa-

164

thers, much of which we reviewed in the last chapter. King's version of the master story includes these events (p. 159): (1) Jesus reveals the pure doctrine to the apostles; (2) the apostles apportion the world among themselves to take the gospel to the world; and (3) Satan challenges the church with weeds in the divine wheat field of the church that lead to wrong belief. In addition, Constantine was the patron of Christianity and convened Nicea to define orthodoxy.

King's assessment of the master story is as follows:

While the plot of the master story presents a powerful and compelling — if problematic — paradigm for religious belief, it is poor history. First of all, the story is incomplete and noticeably slanted. The roles of women, for example, are almost completely submerged from view. In the master story, the male Jesus selects male disciples who pass on tradition to male bishops. Yet we know that in the early centuries and throughout Christian history, women played prominent roles as apostles, teachers, preachers, and prophets. Moreover, the use of terms like "orthodoxy" and "heresy" immediately desig-

165

nates who were the winners and losers, but in practice "heresy" can only be identified by hindsight, instituting the norms of a later age as the standard for an earlier period. Hence the logic is circular: the New Testament and the Nicene Creed define orthodox Christianity, not only in the fourth century and beyond, but anachronistically in the previous centuries as well.

One consequence of the triumph of Nicene orthodoxy was that the viewpoints of other Christians were largely lost, surviving only in documents denouncing them. Until now. The clearest contribution of the recent discoveries is in providing a wealth of primary works that illustrate the plural character of early Christianity and offer alternative voices. They disclose a much more diverse Christianity than we ever suspected; for the later story presents only two kinds of Christians: True Christians (the orthodox) and false Christians (the heretics). We know that the real situation was more complex. Not stark contrasts, but multiple levels of intersection and disjuncture best define the situation . . . And just as the master story functioned to authorize the particular theology and practices of what later came to be orthodoxy, the invention of Gnosticism and Jewish Christianity by modern scholars continues that process in our own time. (pp. 160–61)

Here is the "new" school perspective, what some have called the Neo-Gnostics. Here in more scholarly form is what Dan Brown has placed in his novel. Recent discoveries have unlocked a whole new world. What the citation does not tell you, and what I have tried to show you, is that these views in these texts were neither new nor unknown. Centuries ago the church fathers presented their opponents' views with remarkable accuracy. King claims that Gnosticism is a modern invention, yet the texts we cited indicate that *gnosis* was a driving force behind these texts. She is right that the situation in the first few centuries was more complex than we tend to think, but to minimize the conflict between the schools is to ignore too many ancient texts.

Yet another key representative of this school of study is Helmut Koester. In many ways, he is responsible for giving impetus to this new school and training many who hold to this new view. Another Harvard professor, he wrote *Ancient Christian Gospels* in

1990. That the term *Gnostic* is not used in his title is noteworthy. He claims in his preface that disputes existed in the middle first century between these groups, but that a term such as *orthodox* should be avoided for the first two centuries (p. xxx). Koester argues that elements of the theology of these rejected groups that Tertullian claimed were late cannot be shown to be such. For Koester:

> the earliest gospel traditions and gospel writings contain seeds of both, later heresy as well as later orthodoxy. For the description of the history and development of gospel literature in the earliest period of Christianity, the epithets "heretical" and "orthodoxy" are meaningless. Only dogmatic prejudice can assert that the canonical writings have an exclusive claim to apostolic origin and thus to historical priority." (p. xxx)

A Candid Look at the New School and Its Claims

If these claims were not in scholarly books, we might be tempted to call them hype. Here we see the roots of *The Da Vinci Code* and its real, ultimate argument. The claim is that Christianity needs a new story because the old one was bad history in which the suppressed losers were denied a hearing. Injustice needs correcting. We need to look at the evidence from a fresh historical angle to save those who have not been able to speak for themselves throughout the centuries. *The Da Vinci Code*'s discussion about the alleged historical distortion from the early Christians has made this piece of fiction strike a raw nerve with many Christian readers. In effect, the ancient church is called a liar.

These claims have raised questions for others who do not know this history at all, whether in the Gospels, the master story, or in its newly advertised, revised form. And note who is guilty here. It is not merely the bishops of the past. An entire stream of modern scholarship is at fault because it has dared to discuss these texts in detail and label them Gnostic, non-Christian, and/or heretical. The charge from this new school of study is that the old school's labeling of these texts is an invalid, modern invention. This labeling is a modern tool of the powerful to keep the oppressed at bay. *The Da Vinci Code* seeks to destroy this master story supported by a whole array of scholars present and past. The master story is wrong

169

and needs revision. The author of the novel can call to his aid some big guns of recent scholarship.

But as we discussed before, the best evidence of early Christianity comes not from those of the fourth century and beyond looking back, but from people *in the debate at the time.* These second- and third-century texts were written before Nicea ever happened. There is no circular argument here but an ancient, contemporary contention for ideas. People on both sides of the debate cared deeply about and disagreed about those ideas. Some cared so deeply that they gave their lives as martyrs because they believed they were upholding the truth.

No amount of revisionism can deny that a real debate about the nature of Christianity flourished in the second and third centuries, long before Nicea. Neither can it deny that although these four Gospels had not yet been fully received into a named canon, the four Gospels had risen to the top of the heap in terms of use and influence, and all sides had to deal with them.

Scholarship like that represented by Koester and King has been vigorously challenged. Martin Hengel, emeritus professor of New Testament and early Judaism at the University of Tübingen in Germany, challenges Koester's reading of early Christian history in his work, *The Four Gospels and the One Gospel of Jesus Christ* (2000). He counters and rejects Koester's claim that the nonapostolic gospels existed alongside the four Gospels. Hengel also rejects the idea that the orthodox took the name *gospel* from Gnostic works like those by Marcion. Hengel notes that the Gnostic works imitated the Gospels in claiming to have apostolic roots because they maintained that they had a level of "apostolic authority" (p. 59). Hengel elaborates on this earlier observation and says, "Koester stands things on their head" (p. 247, n. 247). Hengel calls Koester's views about the second-century insignificance of the four Gospels "no less questionable conjectures" (p. 231, n. 144).

Hengel's work defends the early apostolic roots of the gospel tradition and the early establishment of four Gospels. He also defends the fact that the superscriptions (that is, the titles attached to manuscripts of the four Gospels) occur with such consistency that they were in place in the second century. The Gospels did not circulate anonymously, nor were these names a reaction to Gnostic works, as Koester claims. In what is a rebuke to the new school Hengel remarks:

Let those who deny the great age and therefore basically the originality of the Gospel superscriptions in order to preserve their "good" critical conscience, give a better explanation of the completely unanimous and relatively early attestation of these titles, their origin and the names of the authors associated with them. Such an explanation has yet to be given, and it never will be . . . The four-gospel collection did not result from the attempt to defend the "apostolic" Jesus tradition against his [Marcion's] radical attack. It was the other way around. (p. 55)

Some of this debate reviews points we investigated in Code 5, but the issue now focuses not on the history of the past but on how some modern scholarship is trying to reshape and distort that history. You should not get the impression that the "new" school has the facts on its side. That conclusion is very much debated and very much in doubt.

What Use Should We Make of the New Gospel Finds?

A few other points before we reexamine

Mary Magdalene. Our investigation has made an effort not to draw too heavily on the New Testament itself, since the claim is that the winners selected these documents. This claim carries with it the implication that the Gospels are tainted evidence. I do not agree, but I have tried to make the case without appealing to them too much. The attempt to break the code has concentrated on those works carrying the debate on each side of the dispute in the generations immediately following the writing of the earliest texts. In this way, we can see the arguments on both sides and hear both sides of the conversation, the historical debate between these early groups striving to define the nature of Christianity. These discoveries help us get a better picture of the complexity of the early church's landscape. These new gospels are important finds, giving us fresh access to voices we have long known were out there. They are worth studying to understand the history of the period.

On What Do the New and Canonical Writings Agree?

Whether these new finds require a rewriting of the master story is an entirely different matter. The only way to rewrite the master story is to privilege the new writings and elevate their weight to a place above the old writings. Ironically the privileging of the old writings has been portrayed as a kind of moral crime. If it is a crime to privilege the old texts, it is a crime to privilege the new as well. In an investigation, all of the evidence is valuable.

The way to understand the history is to show the debate. Both sides agreed on this point: both views cannot be representative of the roots of the Christian faith. The views are too different. *The four Gospels and these other texts do not share the same core, theological view.*

I now turn to the specific claims that these texts make for Mary Magdalene and for the *inclusive* nature of the early church. What do they actually have to say about the leadership of women in the early church? It is time to look at the details of Code 6.

What About Mary and the Leadership of Women?

Another claim in King's book needs study because Mary is offered as an example of women who possessed major leadership roles in the early church. We already saw in Code 1 that Mary Magdalene was said by some in this school to be the first apostle, the "apostle of the apostles." King makes the point this way:

The apostles were considered to be the guarantors of the true teaching of the church, and male bishops continued to be their sole legitimate successors. This male model of discipleship also provided (and continues to provide) a rationale for the exclusion of women from leadership roles, ignoring the presence of women disciples through Jesus' ministry, at the crucifixion, and as the first witnesses to the resurrection (p. 167).

Later she claims, "To be sure, its [*The Gospel of Mary*'s] position on women's leadership is no doubt a factor to its being labeled heresy" (p. 171). Could the role of Mary crumble the church, as Brown's novel claims, and lead to a massive restructuring of Christian history and thought, as King argues? What is the evidence for the role of women early on? King claims that many women were "apostles, teachers, preachers, and prophets" and that the master story shows its bias most vividly in the way women are suppressed in it. Is that claim historical?

1. The Affirmation of Women in the Biblical Materials

Issues related to this topic are more complex than with the other codes we have examined. As I said earlier, some of what *The Da Vinci Code* argues in this area has more merit than other points the novel raises. The responsibility of a good investigator is to go where the evidence leads — and no farther.

Evidence in the very documents that are supposed to perpetrate the suppression actually indicates a tremendous respect for the role of women, although it does not go as far as new code advocates claim.

For example, consider the biblical material written by Luke, the books of Luke and Acts (hereafter Luke-Acts). Ann Graham Brock, author of *Mary Magdalene, The First Apostle: The Struggle for Authority*, argues that Luke-Acts sides with Peter in his supposed battle with Mary while suppressing her role (pp. 70–71). However, this book notes that the four virgin daughters of Philip were prophets (Acts 21:9), and it presents in a positive light the role of Anna as a prophet rejoicing at Jesus' birth (Luke 2:36–38). Brock's claim about suppression is exaggerated when she discusses Jesus' appearance to Mary. According to Brock, Mary as a witness of Resurrection is demoted in Luke-Acts from her commission to tell the apostles about the Resurrection. She argues that this commission is found in Matthew, Mark, and John, but removed by Luke.

Luke presented Mary, along with several other women, telling the disciples of the empty tomb and announcing the Resurrection. As Luke often did in his work, he did not label an action with a saying but simply described its taking place within the action of the story. In a canon supposedly selected to shut women out, the role of women is affirmed. If the canon had really sought to suppress the role of women, then it would have removed all evidence that women were the first to hear about Jesus' resurrection, something none of the four Gospels do because they seek to tell the story truthfully, even if it runs against the cultural grain of the first century. These texts affirm women, especially when seen against the background we examined in Codes 2 and 3 about first-century views of women. The question is the nature of that affirmation.

Nothing shows this affirmation more than the Resurrection accounts. The story of the four Gospels stands in contrast to the culture around them, which did not regard women as reliable enough to be witnesses.

All four Gospels insist that Jesus first appeared to women. This detail, running against the larger, ancient culture as it does, is one of the key evidences that these Resurrection stories were not invented by a church trying to give Jesus a higher status than He really had. Had believers merely invented these appearance-and-empty-tomb stories with the hope that they would convince the culture about Jesus, they would not have unanimously picked women to bear the story's burden to be true. That Jesus selected women as the first witnesses to God's great act is an affirmation of their value and merit before God.

Our earlier examination of Mary and the role of women highlighted how Jesus affirmed the right of women to be disciples, as shown by the scene with Martha and Mary (Luke 10:38–42), not to mention the role of Mary Magdalene, Susanna, and Joanna as supporters and travel companions with Jesus and the disciples (Luke 8:1–3).

Acts also portrays Priscilla with her husband, Aquila, teaching another proclaimer of the gospel, Apollos, about the faith more exactly (Acts 18:26). So women taught in certain settings, proclaimed the gospel, and were prophets, even in the canonical material. According to these alleged "suppression" texts, it is also likely that deaconesses existed (1 Tim. 3:11). Given that the culture of the time gave women a secondary status, all of this is significant.

2. Biblical Evidence of Limitations of the Role of Women

Limitations on roles should be noted, however, since all the evidence counts. Jesus selected the Twelve, and not one of them was a woman. This point is perhaps the most relevant for our current discussion. The Twelve were not an invention of the later church or bishops to place authority exclusively in the hands of men. The texts noting the Twelve predate the bishops by about a century. What argues for the historical role and reality of Jesus choosing the Twelve is that Jesus' betrayer, Judas, was among them. Had the later church invented this group, would it have chosen to put Judas of Iscariot among them and suggest that Jesus' choice was problematic? Had leaders of the church invented the Twelve, then why did they not tell us far more about many of them, most of whom we know only by name in these materials? The selection of the Twelve represents, in part, a key group of disciples whom Jesus appointed to pass on His tradition.

This limitation also shows up in Acts 1:15–26, when a then dead Judas was replaced with Matthias. The qualifications for the role of apostle in its most technical sense of the Twelve were that the person (1) be male, (2) be with Jesus from the beginning, and (3) be a witness to the Resurrection. The Twelve formed the base of the careful passing on of Jesus' teaching, itself a root and example of the way the Christian faith was passed on. In other words, these texts were part of a carefully recalled and passed on tradition. These texts predate Nicea by 250 years.

3. What Can Be Said in General About the Role of Women Found in the Bible?

Jesus and those around Him did affirm and elevate the role of women, especially in regard to the ancient culture's standard of treating them as second-class citizens. We saw evidence of the culture's giving women a second-class status in earlier citations of "nonpolitically correct" Jewish texts.

But this elevation was not the same as some in our culture claim it was or even wished it had been. Here the charge of being anachronistic can be made against those seeking to establish a new code. Those who suggest that Jesus was a full-fledged feminist (or "the original feminist," as *The Da Vinci Code* says on p. 248) are trying to impose a twenty-first-century standard on first-century evidence. The problem with this description is not that Jesus ignored or devalued women; He did not. He just did not make women an exclusive cause as the term *feminist* implies. Jesus was making the case for the value of *every* human being, not just some. Other texts in 1 Corinthians and the Pastoral Epistles (1 Cor. 11:2–16; 14:33–36; 1 Tim. 2:11–15) assign other limitations to women regarding teaching and speaking in a service for reasons debated by scholars. His followers seemed to be aware of these limitations. The Pastorals appear to limit the role of elders to men. For our purposes, we need not sort out the details of this debate but simply note the likely existence of these limitations. What can be said is that the role of women in the early church was more advanced than in other segments of first-century culture.

4. What About the Charge of Suppression by the Church?

One other point about the suppression of women and the demotion of Mary Magdalene needs attention from the side of the supposed suppressionists. The association

181

of Mary Magdalene with prostitution, a supposed effort to redefine her importance, did not come until A.D. 591 from Pope Gregory the Great. That was a full quarter of a millennium after Nicea! Not only that, but the Eastern Orthodox Church never accepted this portrayal of Mary. If it was a conspiracy, the alleged effort to demote women was very slow to hatch, and those at Nicea showed up way too early to be a part. If there was a conspiracy, some never signed on. A much more likely explanation of Gregory's conclusion, as noted already, was that he confused two women named Mary and saw the anointing as one event. The likelihood of a malicious motive here is not great. When the exalted role of Mary, the mother of Jesus, is added to the discussion, then it is clear that there was no full suppression of women in the early church, although it is true that women in roles of leadership was a source of controversy at certain points in the early church's history.

The objection may come that a conclusion stating that the early church affirmed women but in a manner less than some might wish for today ignores the key evidence. That evidence shows a more open approach by some early Christians. Those other texts indicate that this status was a

182

matter of debate. We look to this question next.

But What About Mary, the Apostle to the Apostles?

The description of Mary as "the apostle to the apostles" is important. In her book *Mary Magdalene, The First Apostle*, Ann Graham Brock argues that the early church phrase "the apostle to the apostles" should be translated "apostle of the apostles" (p. 161, n. 2). She suggests that this means Mary is "foremost" of the apostles because she gets this revelation of the resurrection of Jesus first. Is this correct? Does this one phrase carry all of this significance?

1. Mary the Apostle in the Church Father Hippolytus

In fact, as noted in Code 1, the phrase "apostle of the apostles" does not come from Hippolytus (ca. 170–236). The phrase itself appears much later, in the tenth century. Hippolytus did describe Mary as a female apostle. He did so as a church father who was among those making the case for orthodoxy, that is, from the alleged suppressionist camp! However, he did so grouping her with a set of women who had

183

seen the raised Jesus. More than a century before Nicea, he described the events that made Mary one of the female apostles. Here is the text again: "Lest the female apostles doubt the angels, Christ himself came to them so that the women would be apostles of Christ and by their obedience rectify the sin of ancient Eve . . . Christ showed himself to the (male) apostles and said to them: . . . 'It is I who appeared to these women and I who wanted to send them to you as apostles.' " She received this qualification and title because she saw the Lord and He commissioned her to tell the disciples about His resurrection. This event is one that the Gospels themselves tell us.

Also remember that Mary was not singled out here by herself. Mary was part of a group of women who had this honor. Thus, strictly speaking, the singling out of Mary is something imposed on this passage. She was "an apostle among the apostles," but she was one of a few "female apostles" for Hippolytus.

The term *apostle* had various senses in the early church. In one sense, it referred to a formal role of significant leadership within the church, like the Twelve possessed and as Paul and Barnabas received (Acts 14:14; Rom. 1:1). In another, it had a more general meaning of "one commissioned by another," a sent one who represented another. This term could point to someone who planted churches, engaged in evangelism in new areas as one commissioned to preach and represent Jesus and His message, or to some other unspecified but commissioned leadership role. All believers were commissioned to preach and share about Jesus, but apostles seem to look at a role where the church is represented through what is being done. In all likelihood, the reference to Junia as an apostle in Romans 16:7 was made in this second sense. (Some debate whether Junia was a man or a woman; the latter is quite possible. If she was a woman, then she was an apostle, but in the sense that Paul, in this section of Romans, was greeting a whole array of workers in the church. In fact, she likely helped lead the church in some unspecified role and did so in a manner called noteworthy.) Such apostles were engaged in the serious mission of sharing the gospel and developing new believing communities, but we do not know if her ministry focused on women or if it was more general in its scope. It is unlikely Junia saw the risen Lord, so whatever her role is, it appears distinct from how the title was applied to Mary and others like her who saw

185

the Lord. It could well be that the experience of having seen the risen Lord or having received the announcement of the empty tomb gave Mary and those with her a special "commission" or an apostleship tied to the affirmation that Jesus Christ was alive and had truly been raised by God from the dead. In a real sense, Jesus had sent them to proclaim a very special message that they had experienced.

This overview of the term *apostle* reveals that Hippolytus affirmed the role of women as apostles in a sense. He rooted such a role in Jesus' teaching by appeal to the Resurrection scene. However, after the appearance, Mary was sharing core elements of the gospel by announcing the reality of the Resurrection. Every believer, male and female, was called to share the gospel and testify to this reality, but she had been one of the very few to see evidence of it directly. In other words, she was the "sent one" to the "sent ones." This emphasis is not to make a point about her rank being above those to whom she proclaimed the Resurrection or to give her an official role in the church, but to affirm that women also had the right to declare what God had accomplished through Jesus. In this less technical sense Mary was "an apostle to the apostles." She performed the role of messenger about a core element of the message, the Resurrection.

2. Mary in the *Gospel of Mary*

One more text remains, one noted earlier. In the *Gospel of Mary*, Peter challenged Mary and seemed jealous of her having received a revelation from the risen Jesus. Does this show that women and men faced off in the early church and give evidence that some wanted to rank Peter under Mary?

In the text, Mary received a revelation from Jesus after His resurrection, without the knowledge of Peter and others. She passed on this revelation to them. The content of this revelation, *Gospel of Mary* 9, was not merely that Jesus was raised but teaching about the ascension of the soul. Peter was incredulous that he had been bypassed, while Mary was hurt that Peter reacted in such a way. Levi stepped in and rebuked the hot-tempered Peter. The gospel ended happily ever after with Levi or all preaching the good news (there are two manuscripts of this gospel, one ends with Levi preaching; the other version says "they started going out to teach and preach").

We have noted that these extrabiblical texts are more symbolic than historical.

Karen King says of the *Gospel of Philip* and its famous kiss passage, "*The Gospel of Philip* again offers literal images — kissing and jealousy — in order to interpret them spiritually" (p. 146). I agree with her analysis here and extend it to the *Gospel of Mary*, as this is characteristic of these mystery texts. The conflict portrayed between Peter and Mary pictures the conflict in the early church. Peter, who represented the forces of orthodoxy, refused to accept that God could work with another group, apart from him (that is, the believers who accepted secret knowledge). Mary in her role as the "underdog" female represented those who accepted secret knowledge. In fact, this description may well acknowledge that this Gnostic group was in the minority or that the group lacked persuasive power. The claim is that she did receive revelation from God, even though Peter (read orthodoxy) could not believe it. This gospel ends with Mary affirmed and Peter rebuked.

What is important to understand about this reading of the *Gospel of Mary* is that the story is not about Peter and Mary at all or about gender roles. They symbolize the dispute over revelation. This reading confirms our earlier breaking of the code about the secret gospels. It confirms that the real fight was about who receives revelation from God and who can speak to what Christianity is. Modern readers, seekers after a new code and story, have reversed the imagery and turned the text into one about gender roles.

What Can We Say About Mary Magdalene and Gender Roles in the Early Church?

The history of the early church shows us that women were elevated to a new and significant position by Jesus and His followers. This elevation, however, may not reach the modern standards of some, even though there is an effort by some to fudge the evidence to make it say more than it does. Mary Magdalene and other women were significant disciples and privileged to be the first to see and hear from the risen Jesus. Yet none of our evidence, even the texts that some wish to bring forward, indicates a gender conflict or a suppression related to gender. The conflict portrayed in these texts between Peter and Mary was not over gender but over access to revelation among competing groups. Those who argued for secret revelation in their time portrayed themselves as an emotionally abused female

(Mary Magdalene) suffering at the hands of a hot-tempered male (Peter). The claim that gender issues drive these passages misreads and overreads these texts. There was no conspiracy against women by male bishops. It was a dispute over the meaning of Christianity. It was a debate over whether older written sources or more recent, revelatory contents helped people identify and define this faith.

I am not a Roman Catholic. Nor am I seeking to defend the Roman church or the primacy of Peter. I write as one who has given his life to the study of the New Testament and the early church. Our investigation has sought to present the key evidence and witnesses in order to examine how much substance there is to the claims of facts within *The Da Vinci Code*. At stake is an adequate historical and cultural understanding of the Christian faith.

We are almost finished. Our investigation has taken us to ancient texts; now we have to sort through and analyze modern disputes. We have broken Code 6. Mary Magdalene was affirmed in her role as witness to the Resurrection, although she was not given an office in the church for that role.

In the midst of our examination of the role of Mary, we found out something even more interesting concerning our discussion of Christianity and culture. We have exposed behind *The Da Vinci Code* and the "secret" code of the Gnostic writings to which it appeals a megacode. *The Da Vinci Code* is not a mere work of fiction dressed in the clothes of quasi nonfiction. It reflects an effort to represent and, in some cases, rewrite history with a selective use of ancient evidence that it ironically claims was the failing of the old story. It reflects an effort to redefine one of the key cultural forces standing at the base of Western civilization, the Christian faith. It claims to expose as fact something that is not there. Though there are a few points to be made and appreciated from such study, most of what lies at the base of this megacode lacks substantive historical support. In breaking *The Da Vinci Code* we have discovered there is much more going on here than the creation of an entertaining novel — there is a revision of what Christianity was and is. It is virtual reality at work.

We have two codes left to examine. One is raised by the novel, and the other is a new look at the topic the novel addresses. Given what we have uncovered so far, do the Holy Grail and the Sion Priory have anything left to tell us? What is the remaining relevance

191

of *The Da Vinci Code*? We turn now to Code 7, our summary code, where we review what our investigation shows and ask, Where do we go from here?

Code 7

WHAT IS THE REMAINING RELEVANCE OF *THE DA VINCI CODE?*

The "Great Cover-Up" Claims of *The Da Vinci Code*

The Da Vinci Code uses the words of Teabing to give an assessment of what might be called the Great Cover-Up (pp. 253–54): "Leonardo is not the only one who has been trying to tell the world the truth about the Holy Grail. The royal bloodline of Jesus Christ has been chronicled in exhaustive detail by scores of historians." In the novel's subsequent listing of these historical works after this quotation, *Holy Blood, Holy Grail* is given the prime place. That work, as we noted at the start of our investigation, is described in the novel as the "best-known tome" and an "international bestseller." Although stating that the book and its three authors "made some dubious leaps of faith," the character Teabing concludes his assessment of that book by saying, "Their fundamental premise

193

is sound, and . . . they finally brought the idea of Christ's bloodline into the mainstream." Teabing continues, "This was a secret the Vatican had tried to bury in the fourth century . . . The Church, in order to defend itself against the Magdalene's power, perpetuated her image as a whore and buried evidence of Christ's marriage to her, thereby defusing any potential claims that Christ had a surviving bloodline and was a mortal prophet." Near the end of the discussion, Langdon says the historical evidence for this is "substantial."

The Foundational Claims of *The Da Vinci Code* Found Lacking

We have examined this claim and found it wanting historically at every key point. Mary Magdalene was not married to Jesus. Jesus was not married to anyone else. He had no children. Jesus was single in a manner that Jews of His time could appreciate. Jesus, as a religious Jew, could be single.

The secret gospels do not tell us very much new about the centuries just after Christ, other than to make clear that they contain a distinct theology from the biblical books, to show that the church fathers who described their views did so accurately, and to let us hear them present their views in their own words. The secret gospels noted in the novel were part of a contentious dispute among various Christian factions about who spoke best for Jesus and Christianity. These gospels, written after the four Gospels of the New Testament, claimed access to revelation from God independent of the writings that many in the church regarded as authoritative and as a reflection of the church's most historic tradition. The presence of such views fueled the formal recognition of the canon, a process completed in the fourth century.

The deity of Jesus was not a creation of a fourth-century vote or council but is based on the teaching of the four Gospels and other New Testament books. These four canonical Gospels are rooted in apostolic tradition, and they were firmly established as the defining texts of the Christian church by the end of the second century, if not earlier.

Mary Magdalene was not a prostitute, but neither was that description part of an act of suppression. Mary was affirmed in her role as a witness to the Resurrection, a role that made her among the first to announce the Resurrection to the eleven remaining apostles. In that sense, she was an "apostle to the apostles." The dispute of the early Christian

195

centuries was not primarily about gender or gender roles, but about theology, namely, views about God, Jesus, salvation, spirituality, and revelation. The historical foundation for almost all of what *The Da Vinci Code* claims is not substantive.

In all of this, *The Da Vinci Code* fails to deliver on its claim that its skeleton is historical. If the foundation of its argument about Jesus being married and having a bloodline is this thin, then all the subsequent history it relates becomes irrelevant. All the theories attached to the Sion Priory, the Knights Templar, Opus Dei, and the Merovingian line tied to a bloodline of Jesus fall to the side. There is no good historical reason to discuss these later groups in relationship to a theory about Jesus whose foundation is lacking. These groups did exist and they have a history that is fascinating in its own right, but they do not have any connection to issues about a bloodline from Jesus. (As an introduction to these groups in their most general terms, I have supplied a brief discussion of each of them in the Glossary. For details, study the works of medieval or modern historians, depending on the group.) Of one thing our study is absolutely certain: whatever Mary Magdalene is, she is no Holy Grail with a trail of royal descendants from Jesus.

What Can We Say About What Remains of *The Da Vinci Code*?

Two historical claims of the novel stand: (1) women were elevated by what Jesus taught (although probably not as much as some would suggest), and (2) Mary Magdalene was not a prostitute. The remaining foundation of the novel is made of sand. The dots do not connect historically. The breaking of Code 7, the summary code, is that there is no basis for theorizing about the Holy Grail as Mary Magdalene, a Merovingian line that goes back to Jesus, a Sion Priory that has a reason to exist, or any cover-up involving Opus Dei. Whatever those groups were or are, they cannot have been involved in a story that had anything to do with the descendants of Jesus. Fiction is fiction, and readers should appreciate it as such.

What Can We Say About the Code Behind *The Da Vinci Code* and the New Scholarship That Fuels It?

As we pursued some of the ideas and texts presented in *The Da Vinci Code*, we surfaced another, second layer of discussion, some of which the novel appealed to and embellished. *Holy Blood, Holy Grail* also appealed to such works. Those ideas are rooted in academic treatments of early Christian history up to the fourth century. Our investigation brought in many of the most prominent studies in discussing topics like the secret gospels and Mary Magdalene. The studies come from some of the most prestigious institutions in the United States, generating interest on national TV and in magazines. The studies date up to 2003 and reflect work that has been going on for about the last half century. Some points made in these studies have enhanced our appreciation for the complexity and diversity of the Christian movement in the second to fourth centuries. These treatments are not as undisciplined or sloppy as *The Da Vinci Code*, and so are more important. They also seek to make the case for a reconfiguration of Christian understanding, involving serious study of significant ancient texts.

Such study is not immune to critical assessment. In the process of examining *The Da Vinci Code*, we have had reason to look at aspects of this study of the roots of the Christian faith. We have engaged its rationale, agenda, and plausibility. We have raised major questions about this "new" school that is calling for a new story about the Christian faith. Although clothed in fine garb, many points argued in these works were found lacking.

In some ways, this is a more important finding than the critical assessment of a best-selling novel that elaborated on and embellished these more academic ideas. Popular and cultural beliefs often emerge out of what the culture comes to embrace as top-drawer scholarship, and the claims of *The Da Vinci Code* are a prime example of such a phenomenon. Part of the goal of our investigation has been to examine *The Da Vinci Code* (the popular expression) and to make clear what actually stands behind significant parts of it (the academic scholarship).

Why Break the Da Vinci Code?

This brief analysis of *The Da Vinci Code*'s fictional, albeit entertaining, treatment of Christianity's roots and history cannot do full justice to the complexity of the topic. However, it can clarify the outlines of the substantive debate, past and present. Our investigation has been an exercise in historical appreciation; that is why so many ancient texts have dotted our journey, like road signs directing the way.

This work also has sought to give a sense of why such discussions matter. Knowing the history and the complex factors that have shaped that history are important when we consider who God is, what people believe, why they believe it, and why institutions like the church are structured as they are. Identifying what is *not* a part of that history is a useful exercise. Sometimes the claim is made that such discussions about religious issues are all "a matter of faith" or "people just have different opinions" on such topics. However, in moving toward faith and in coming to opinions it is crucial to have the facts lined up as clearly as possible or as best as we can assemble them. The Christian faith has always claimed at its base that there are genuine events of history tied to its teaching. Suggestions, such as the novel makes, that such ideas are creations of adherents three centuries after the fact are not minor details; they are core assertions about what Christianity was and is. Understanding the nature of this debate and the factors that feed it is important. Understanding who we were and why helps us appreciate who we are and maybe even who we should be.

Our study has sought to raise meaningful

questions about an entire strand of scholarship now making it big on the airwaves as well as in bookstores and on newsstands. We have raised serious questions about the cogency of many of its most important historical claims, even though such ideas emanate from some of our greatest halls of learning. To make people aware of what is taking place within the study of Christianity places us all in a better position to assess what is being claimed. Our investigation makes no claims to revelation; it is committed to disclosure and discussion. There is no reason why debates in ivory towers should not also take place at water coolers.

The significance of the topic can hardly be exaggerated. I hope that the journey has been worth it. Perhaps the discussion of the roots of faith can proceed with a fresh awareness of where the lines have been and are being drawn. Behind the discussion swirling around works like *The Da Vinci Code* is not just the solving of a murder mystery or a conspiracy theory, but the pursuing of basic questions of religious inquiry and longing that stand at the heart of self-understanding and, more important, relationship with God.

That question leaves us with one more code to discuss. It examines the figure who stands in many ways at the center of the controversy. His legacy was at the center of discussion and debate in *The Da Vinci Code*. One remaining question is, Who was (and is) Jesus, and what can Mary Magdalene tell us about Him?

Code 8

THE REAL JESUS CODE

Examining the Life Code

In many ways, our investigation and analysis are complete. But life is about far more than analyzing the facts. Unlike Sergeant Friday on *Dragnet*, we must acknowledge that there is more to the core issues of life than "just the facts, ma'am." In dealing with this last code, I want to add a personal word about why these issues are worth the time and effort we have put into them, both as an investigator and as one who has taken the time to follow the investigation. There is a very important way in which Jesus and Mary Magdalene intersect that points to real issues of life and relationship with God. To consider that final code, the real Jesus code, I share with you a glimpse of my journey.

There is no mystery greater than life itself. One of the most memorable days of my life was when our first child was born. Just after the birth, I was holding a new human no longer than my forearms. Breathing on her own for the first time was someone alive, alert, and potentially independent. I was amazed at all that goes into life. It is wondrous how everything must come together and work to produce a life, a sacred soul.

Living is not a trivial matter, nor are life's choices. As common as life is, much about it remains shrouded in mystery. We do not know how long we shall live or what the direction of our lives will be. For those of us who are older, it is a mystery to look back on what life has been and examine what has caused a life to go in this or that direction. Many formative events are things we cannot control and whose rationale we do not really understand.

I remember when I first started to think seriously about life and its mystery. It was when my mother was stricken with cancer. I watched her waste away over a six-year period, only to die when I was fourteen years old. That was a mystery to me. That was a code to be cracked. Life was a treasure with a secret contained within itself. As exciting as birth was, death was equally perplexing.

The Divine Jesus Code

What does all of this have to do with a fictional book that contains questionable history? The short answer is, a lot. You see, Mary Magdalene was a witness to one of the greatest mystery breakers of all time. She witnessed Jesus' resurrection. She witnessed Jesus' life. In reflecting on the beginning of Jesus' life, Christians declare that Jesus was the unique, promised One born to Mary and Joseph by the power of God's Spirit (Matthew and Luke). He was the One whom John the Baptist preached about, who clears the way to God (Mark), even the sent One from God and from the side of God (John). In the various ways that the four Gospels introduce the story of Jesus and in the different emphases, there is one key and common point: Jesus uniquely reveals and stands at the center of what God did and does for humanity. At the center of that story stand Jesus' death and ultimately His resurrection. That Resurrection event, picturing as it does the breakout of life from death, is the real code to understand. In reflecting on the Resurrection, Christians declare that God made a vindicating statement about who Jesus is, where life is, and where life goes.

When we investigated the life of Mary Magdalene, we noted how it was against all historical logic to believe that the church made up the story of women being the first to see Jesus. Culturally in the first century, they had no persuasive role as witnesses. In other words, the unique event itself created the testimony. That unique event points to a unique person. But then that observation leads to the question, What does the resurrection of Jesus mean?

In short, Jesus' resurrection is the collision of death with life, and life wins! But this is not an abstract engagement of life with death, or a depiction of everyone's life and death. It is the power of God working creatively to renew life in One who had died but made certain claims about God, Himself, and life. Jesus preached that the kingdom of God came with and through Him. That kingdom involves in part a presence and rule of God that bring such order to living that life can become what it was designed to be. Jesus claimed that as the *Son,* He must return to the *Father* so that God could give the *Spirit* to those who embraced what Jesus was saying. A reading of John 14–16 explains that promise. Jesus called this kingdom teaching a mystery, not in the sense of secrets for insiders, because Jesus preached that message openly on the streets and in the countryside. He often preached and then said, "Let the one who has ears to hear, hear." The mystery is for those who will hear it. It is a secret lost for those who will not listen.

Jesus also said, "I have come that they might have life, and have it abundantly" (John 10:10 NET). In all of this Jesus was bringing a kind of decoding to the mystery of life, life lived consciously in the presence of God. That does not mean that every question about why things happen receives an answer. Nor does it mean that life becomes problem free or less enigmatic. It does mean that life begins to make sense because Jesus gives access and understanding to what real life is.

Part of decoding that mystery involves understanding who we are without God and appreciating why we need God. Theologians use the word *sin* to describe our problem. It is not a popular word in our culture. I often suggest that to see what it means, we just need to read the daily newspaper. Most of us, if we are honest, understand that often we act and react in ways that are destructive to ourselves and others. Sin is not about pointing a finger at others; sin is about understanding who we are and what our tendencies are when we free ourselves from accountability to the living, Creator God. There may be no greater truth more often denied than that sin lives powerfully in our world — and we are powerless in ourselves to deal with it.

Such discussion is not about shame, guilt, or seeking what naysayers call a crutch. It is about a real world where people do severe damage to one another and themselves. It is not a world of virtual reality that pretends everything is pretty much okay. It is a world of reality that humbly faces the fact that left to ourselves and our independence, we will act in destructive ways. Our culture, which elevates independence to divinelike status, is not comfortable looking at itself in this kind of mirror. No one is comfortable facing up to this ugly reality of life.

Jesus was comfortable with addressing such issues, with calling us to dependence on God through the work that God was doing through Him. He was comfortable reminding us of our responsibility as beings created by God to love God completely and love others as ourselves as a result. In loving this way and telling us this, Jesus was being honest about the fact that we need to seek divine forgiveness. That is part of the reason He preached, "The time is fulfilled, and the kingdom of God is at hand; repent, and believe in the gospel [that is, the good news]" (Mark 1:15 RSV).

Jesus not only preached about God; Jesus put His life where His words were. In the famous meal scene painted by Leonardo da Vinci, *The Last Supper,* Jesus declared what His life mission was about: "This is my body which is given for you . . . This cup which is poured out for you is the new covenant in my blood" (Luke 22:19–20 RSV). Jesus came to die so that we might understand the mystery of life and live before God in the way that the Creator designed life to be lived. Jesus came to show us how seriously God took sin and the restoration to life. Jesus also came to show that God loved us so much that God would give up a precious life into death so that we could experience life. And then God would take up that life into new life to show that life was about more than merely existing on earth. God provided unbroken fellowship with Him through the sent One God loved, God's unique Son. That is the message of the apostolic testimony found in the New Testament.

God took sin so seriously that He offered the One He loved and sent Him to take up sin on our behalf in order to point the way to life. When God raised Jesus, God was saying "Amen" to that mission and message, as well as to the person Jesus claimed to be. Jesus' death and resurrection say that through Jesus, God provides the way to life that includes the understanding that sin is a blot on our lives. We also understand that if we are to see the way to true or full life, God must show it to us. The way out of the mysterious darkness that encumbers life when we live it independently of God is to take the path God shows through the code breaker, Jesus. The way out includes admitting our need for God and for forgiveness. We were created to be dependent upon God. The way out is to acknowledge what God has said about us through the message of Jesus' work for us, that is, through the provision for forgiveness and life that Jesus made through His own sacrifice and death for us.

The church has called this acknowledgment faith. It is faith in Jesus the Savior. It is a faith that saves because it embraces life as God created it to be. This faith receives life as a gracious gift that God makes available to us through the way Jesus has made. Faith in God through Jesus is the most important message the church preaches because it is the good news of the way to life. Such faith understands who we are and our failure independent of God. Such faith appreciates our need to know Him, and the power of life that comes through acknowledging what Jesus' death and resurrection tell us about God, ourselves, and life. Such faith confesses not only sin but also the need for forgiveness and life.

Such faith turns one's life into an expression of gratitude for the opportunity to fellowship with God. Such faith knows that God's acceptance of us was rooted in God's own selfless act of sacrifice and love. Such faith is open to God's leading, direction, and instruction that come through Jesus and the messengers He instructed. Those closest to Jesus have told us Jesus' story. That is why to understand the code breaker and the real code, we must read their story, for their story is also our story.

What Mary Magdalene Tells Us

Where does Mary Magdalene come in? How is her story ours? One sad morning, Mary Magdalene and a group of women journeyed to a tomb to anoint what they expected to be the lifeless remains of One they had hoped would be their deliverer. They had no idea that the tomb would be empty. Just imagine how she felt, having had her hopes dashed that perhaps Jesus was the One from God that generations had hoped would come to deliver them. I can imagine her thinking through the time she had spent with Jesus, when He exorcised the demons from her or maybe when she sat at His feet listening to Him teach about God and His will. Perhaps she pondered what she had seen a few days before, Jesus hanging from a cross, still asking that those who sent Him there be forgiven. No one really knows what she thought about as she journeyed with some of her friends to anoint what she expected to be a corpse. But surely thoughts about the One she had followed were in her soul.

Whatever she was thinking, everything in her world changed when she reached the tomb. She got the surprise of her life that also was the surprise of life. The tomb had no human remains. Jesus was alive. God had raised Jesus to new life to show the way to life. Jesus, the real risen Jesus, showed Himself to be the code breaker. Out of the mystery of death had come life because God had broken the code through Jesus.

Mary Magdalene was not the wife of Jesus. She was a disciple of Jesus who points the way. To break the Da Vinci Code is to ask questions about who Jesus really was —

and is. To break that second, more important code leads to fellowship and life with God through Jesus. As a witness to the Resurrection and as one among the first to see and understand what God had done through Jesus, Mary Magdalene serves us far better as a disciple of Jesus than as Jesus' alleged wife. Out of a death for sin comes the opportunity of new and resurrected life with God. God says simply, "Believe in Him. Trust in the work He has done and will do for you." What lies ahead of such an embrace of faith is a new and unending life of fellowship with God lived through God's forgiveness and spiritual provision. That is the real Jesus code. That is something worth believing.

ABOUT THE AUTHOR

Darrell L. Bock is Research Professor of New Testament Studies at Dallas Theological Seminary in Dallas, Texas. He also serves as Professor for Spiritual Development and Culture for the Seminary's Center for Christian Leadership. His special fields of study involve hermeneutics, the use of the Old Testament in the New, Luke-Acts, the historical Jesus, and gospels studies. As well as being a corresponding editor for Christianity Today and past President of the Evangelical Theological Society, Bock serves as an elder at Trinity Fellowship Church in Richardson, Texas, where he lives with his wife, Sally, and their three children.

ACKNOWLEDGMENTS

This investigation is a response to hundreds of questions I have been asked over the last year about *The Da Vinci Code*. My thanks go to Thomas Nelson, and especially to Jonathan Merkh, for proposing this idea, and to Brian Hampton, Kyle Olund, Dimples Kellogg, and Elizabeth Kea for their fine editorial advice. Thanks also go to my wife, Sally, and to two of my sisters-in-law, Martha Sheeder and Elizabeth Volmert. They read the novel and had many questions about it. Their encouragement was a major motivation for writing this work. I wrote it for them and many others like them who just wanted to know what was going on historically with the claims of the novel. A special note of appreciation goes to Kathy Wills. She had the original idea for this book and proposed it to Thomas Nelson. I am grateful to Father Frank Moloney for his willingness to write a Foreword and explain how many other academics from a context distinct from my own see these issues. I also wish to thank

Jeanmarie Condon and her staff at ABC News, including Yael Lavie and Elizabeth Vargas. They made me aware of the cultural impact of this novel and offered me the invitation to address the issue. Finally, my appreciation goes to some colleagues — Richard Taylor, Stephen Sanchez, John Hannah, and Jeffrey Bingham — who read and commented on this material in its early form. Special thanks go to my daughter, Elisa Laird, who also read my draft with a keen eye and with whom I had many phone conversations into the night about the issues raised by the novel and my book. Their evaluation was of immense help.

December 8, 2003

SELECTED BIBLIOGRAPHY

Translations of extrabiblical gospels come from James M. Robinson, ed., *The Nag Hammadi Library*, rev. ed. (San Francisco: HarperSanFrancisco, 1990). In some cases, I cross-checked these translations with other renderings in some works cited below. These translations are a part of the even more comprehensive collection edited by Robinson, *The Facsimile Edition of the Nag Hammadi Codices* (Leiden: E. J. Brill, 1972–1984). This collection has now been reissued in a five-volume paperback set, *The Coptic Gnostic Library: A Complete Edition of the Nag Hammadi Codices* (Leiden: E. J. Brill, 2000), a condensed form of the fourteen-volume hardback edition published between 1975 and 1995. For those seeking to investigate these texts in their earliest discovered form, this is the best source for that material.

Citations from the church fathers come from Alexander Roberts and James Donaldson, eds., with notes by A. Cleveland Coxe, *The Ante-Nicene Fathers: Trans-*

lations of *The Writings of the Fathers Down to A.D. 325.* This is the Eerdmans American edition of this series, which was originally published in 1867–85. This explains the translations' older English flavor.

Baigent, Michael, Richard Leigh, and Henry Lincoln. *Holy Blood, Holy Grail.* New York: Dell Doubleday, 1982.

Bauckham, Richard. *Gospel Women: Studies of the Named Women in the Gospels.* Grand Rapids: Eerdmans, 2002.

Blomberg, Craig. "Book Review of *The Da Vinci Code*: A Novel." *The Denver Journal: An Online Review of Current Biblical and Theological Studies* 7 (2004), www.denverseminary.edu.

Bock, Darrell L. *Blasphemy and Exaltation in Judaism and the Final Examination of Jesus.* Wissenschaftliche Untersuchungen zum Neuen Testament 2 Reihe 106, ed. Martin Hengel and Otto Hofius. Tübingen: Mohr/Siebeck, 1998.

———. "Was Jesus Married to Mary Magdalene? All the Available Evidence

Clearly Points to an Answer of 'No.' " ABCNews.com, November 12, 2003.

Brock, Ann Graham. *Mary Magdalene, The First Apostle: The Struggle for Authority.* Harvard Theological Studies 51. Cambridge, MA: Harvard University Press, 2003.

Brown, Dan. *The Da Vinci Code: A Novel.* New York: Doubleday, 2003.

Crossan, John Dominic. "Why Jesus Didn't Marry." Beliefnet.com, fall 2003.

Hengel, Martin. *The Four Gospels and the One Gospel of Jesus Christ.* Harrisburg: Trinity, 2000.

Hurtado, Larry. *Lord Jesus Christ: Devotion to Jesus in Earliest Christianity.* Grand Rapids: Eerdmans, 2003.

Jansen, Katherine Ludwig. "Mary Magdalena: *Apostolorum Apostola,*" in *Women Preachers and Prophets through Two Millennia of Christianity.* ed. Beverly Mayne Kienzle and Pamela J. Walker. Los Angeles: University of California Press, 1998, pp. 57-95.

Jenkins, Philip. *Hidden Gospels: How the Search for Jesus Lost Its Way*. Oxford: Oxford University Press, 2001.

Jones, F. Stanley, ed. *Which Mary? The Marys of Early Christian Tradition*. Society of Biblical Literature Symposium Series 19, ed. Christopher Matthews. Atlanta: Society of Biblical Literature, 2002.

Kantrowitz, Barbara, and Anne Underwood. "The Bible's Lost Stories." *Newsweek*, December 8, 2003, 48–59.

King, Karen L. *The Gospel of Mary of Magdala: Jesus and the First Woman Apostle*. Santa Rosa, CA: Polebridge Press, 2003.

Koester, Helmut. *Ancient Christian Gospels*. Philadelphia: Trinity Press International, 1990.

Mathewes-Green, Frederica. "What Heresy?" Beliefnet.com, July 12, 2003, and ChristianityToday.com. *Books and Culture*, November–December 2003.

Metzger, Bruce M. *The Canon of the New Testament: Its Origin, Development, and Significance.* Oxford: Clarendon, 1987.

Miesel, Sandra. "Dismantling the Da Vinci Code." *Crisis Magazine,* September 1, 2003.

O'Collins, Gerald, and Daniel Kendall. "Mary Magdalene as Major Witness to Jesus' Resurrection," *Theological Studies* 48 (1987): 631–46.

Pagels, Elaine. *Beyond Belief: The Secret Gospel of Thomas.* New York: Random House, 2003.

———. *The Gnostic Gospels.* New York: Vintage Books/Random House, 1979.

Glossary

This Glossary covers the major themes and figures raised in *Breaking the Da Vinci Code*. Some topics noted here are not covered in much detail in the body of the book but are included because they are mentioned in *The Da Vinci Code*. It is *Breaking the Da Vinci Code*'s argument that the problems of *The Da Vinci Code*'s portrayal of history of the first four centuries render the issues tied to later centuries irrelevant as far as history is concerned. Nonetheless, I have included some of these topics in the Glossary for the sake of completeness. Much of the history of topics related to the medieval period is contested. In fact, most of the alleged connections that go back to that period according to *The Da Vinci Code* are also suspect. It is quite likely that everything about the Priory of Sion, founded in 1956, was a fabrication. A good, short review of many issues tied to the medieval period is the article by Sandra Miesel noted in the Selected Bibliography.

Apocalypse of Peter: A third-century

pseudonymous Christian Gnostic text that treats Jesus as a docetic figure, that is, one who only apparently existed as man and God. This work is a topic of Code 4.

Apocryphon of John: A second-century work of mythological Gnosticism that Irenaeus (see the entry for him) criticized in his work *Against Heresies*. It mentions the existence of the supreme being of pure light from whom emanations like Christ and Sophia (Divine Wisdom often portrayed as a female) come. This work is noted in Code 4.

Arius: A teacher of the early fourth century (d. A.D. 335) who taught that Christ was not completely God and was subordinate to the Father. His view, known as Arianism, was finally condemned at the Council of Constantinople in A.D. 381.

Athanasius: A fourth-century church father (A.D. 295–373) who argued against Arius at Nicea and whose view of Jesus prevailed at that council. He was the first to use the term *canon* and to name the twenty-seven New Testament books most Christians use today.

Canon: A term that means "standard" and refers to the books received as Scripture by the church. These canonical books were recognized by the church over a period of time. The four gospels of Matthew, Mark, Luke, and John were well established in the second century long before Nicea in A.D. 325, as Code 5 argued.

Chalice: A cup. In *The Da Vinci Code*, the chalice is an allegory to protect the true nature of the Holy Grail as Mary Magdalene.

Church Fathers: A shorthand way to refer to the leaders of the church in the first four centuries who followed after the first couple of generations of Christians. They are major figures in discussions of Codes 4 and 5.

Constantine: Emperor of Rome in the early fourth century who converted to Christianity and convened the Council of Nicea in A.D. 325.

Coptic: The language of many of the discovered Gnostic texts.

Demiurge: A Greek term that means "maker" or "builder." It refers to Gnosticism's derivative god responsible for the material creation.

Diatessaron: This second-century work from Tatian, written around A.D. 172, is a single continuous story about Jesus. It is the first harmony of Jesus' life, that is, the first attempt to bring together the various sources being used in the church about

Jesus into one story. The name means "through the four." This reference shows that the four Gospels were well established by the end of the second century. This work is discussed in Code 5.

Diocletian: Roman emperor who in A.D. 303 issued an edict persecuting Christians and ordering that their holy writings were to be burned.

Docetism: The belief that the divine Christ only appeared to be human and only appeared to suffer.

Dualism: See *Gnostics*.

Essenes: A pious Jewish group of the first century. This group is discussed in Codes 2 and 3. Many Essenes were separatists, and some were the likely residents of Qumran, a Jewish community that lived in the wilderness and awaited God's deliverance. The Qumran community dates from the second century B.C. until the defeat of Israel in A.D. 70. The famous Dead Sea Scrolls were found in various caves in Qumran between 1947 and 1956.

Eusebius: Bishop of Caesarea in Palestine (A.D. 269 – ca. 339). A friend of Constantine, he wrote the earliest history of the church, known as the *Ecclesiastical History*.

Fourfold Gospel: The biblical gospels of

Matthew, Mark, Luke, and John. They all date from the first century and are the topic of Code 5.

Gnostics: A "Christian" sect of the second and third centuries that believed in dualism, namely, a distinction between the purity of the immaterial world and the corruptibility of the material world. They also believed that the God of creation was not the pure God, that there was a distinction between Jesus who suffered on the cross and the Christ who was the transcendent Savior. They held that the revelation they received gave them unique insight over any other writings. This revelation provided them with access to *gnosis,* or knowledge about God. This group and those like them constitute the key topic of Code 4.

Gospel of Mary (of Magdala): A Gnostic gospel of the second century. Its discussion of Mary and Peter is examined in Codes 1 and 6.

Gospel of Philip: Another second-century Gnostic gospel noted in Codes 1, 4, and 6. This gospel indicates that Jesus had a special regard for Mary Magdalene.

Gospel of Thomas: An early Gnostic gospel that claims to be a collection of sayings from Jesus. It dates from the early part of the second century. It is a matter of scholarly debate whether many of its sayings actually go back to the time of Jesus. Most likely do not. It is a topic in Codes 4 through 6.

Heresy: A term referring to false teaching that has sufficient error as not to reflect true belief. Codes 4 and 5 deal with issues related to this topic.

Hippolytus: A late second- and early third-century church father. His remarks about Mary Magdalene are treated in Codes 1 and 6.

Holy Grail: *Grail* is a variation of a French word meaning a "dish." The Grail is an unspecified holy object that was the topic of various legends and quests during the first crusades. In Western culture, the quest for the Holy Grail has been a metaphor for the difficult or impossible quest. Between 1180 and 1240, there was an outpouring of stories about it. The Grail, seen in some versions as a cup, was said to hold the blood of the crucified Christ. It was supposedly brought to Britain two thousand years ago. That legend is set in the Arthurian Britain of the sixth century. This form of the legend claimed that Joseph of Arimathea received the Grail from the risen Jesus and that it eventually was brought to Britain. However, some tradition traces the cup of the

Last Supper to a Cathar stronghold in the Pyrenees, under the guardianship of the Knights Templar. As *The Catholic Dictionary* article notes, the medieval Latin word *gradale* became in Old French *graal*, or *greal*, or *greel*, whence the English *grail*. Others derive the word from *garalis* or from *cratalis* (*crater*, a mixing bowl). It certainly means a dish. The explanation of *San greal* as "sang real" (kingly blood) was not current until the later Middle Ages and really has nothing to do with the original legend. Other etymologies that have been advanced may be passed over as obsolete. Because of its association with the Last Supper, it was regarded to have special power according to these legends. The Grail is briefly noted in the Introduction and in the discussion of Codes 1 and 7. In *The Da Vinci Code*, the Grail is actually Mary Magdalene, the symbol for womanhood, the sacred feminine, and the goddess lost (p. 238), the presence of which the church is suppressing, with woman now depicted as the enemy. This has nothing to do with the original legends of the Grail.

Hypostasis of the Archons: A third-century Gnostic text that discusses the Creation and identifies the various deities of Gnostic belief. It is noted in Code 4.

Irenaeus: A second-century church father. His major work is *Against Heresies*. His reaction to the gospels outside of Matthew, Mark, Luke, and John appears in Codes 4 and 5.

Josemaria Escriva: Founder of Opus Dei (see *Opus Dei* below) in 1928.

Justin Martyr: A second-century church father who wrote against Marcion in A.D. 150–60. His key works are the *Dialogue with Trypho* and two apologies, known as *I Apology* and *II Apology*. He is discussed in Code 5.

Knights Templar: A monastic military order formed at the end of the first crusade with the mandate of protecting Christian pilgrims en route to the Holy Land. They were established at some point in A.D. 1118. Never before had a group of secular knights banded together and taken the monastic vows. In this sense they were the first of the Warrior Monks. The Templars fought alongside King Richard I of England (Richard the Lion Hearted or Lion Heart; king 1189–99) and other crusaders in the battles for the Holy Lands. The last of these knights were executed by the pope and other rulers in the years 1307–14. They are briefly noted in Code 7.

Les Dossiers Secrets: Alleged "secret"

documents containing an alleged genealogy of Jesus that the church suppressed. In fact, it seems quite likely that these documents are a complete fabrication. The "dossiers secrets" attempt to present a number of families today — including the Plantards and the Hapsburgs — as being descended from the Merovingians. They also argue that all dynasties since then have implicitly been usurpers due to the pact between Clovis (see *Merovingians* below) and the church. Also allegedly among the documents is a list of "Grand Masters" of a secret society, among whose members is Leonardo da Vinci.

Marcion: A second-century teacher who rejected the influence of Judaism on Christianity and thus argued for an abridged version of Luke as the only true gospel. He also appealed to his own direct revelations. His influence in Christian history is noted in Codes 4 and 5.

Mary Magdalene: A follower of Jesus who was the beneficiary of an exorcism from Jesus. She also witnessed His death, burial, and resurrection. She was among the first to hear of Jesus' resurrection and see the raised Jesus. She was not a prostitute, as some held. She is discussed in Codes 1, 2, and 6.

Merovingians: A dynasty of Frankish kings descended, according to tradition, from Merovech, chief of the Salian Franks, whose son was Childeric I and whose grandson was Clovis I, the founder of the Frankish monarchy. Clovis I died in A.D. 511. The claim that they were descended from Jesus lacks any credible historical evidence, as Codes 1 and 2 show. They were entirely subject to their mayors of the palace, the Carolingians, who became the nominal as well as the actual rulers of the Franks when Pepin the Short deposed (A.D. 751) the last Merovingian king, Childeric III. They are sometimes called "the first race of the kings of France." Their presence ran from the fifth to the eighth centuries. In *The Da Vinci Code* it is alleged that this group of kings is descended from the union of Jesus and Mary. This royal family and the claims about it are briefly noted in Code 7.

Montanus: A second-century teacher who appealed to his own revelation as authoritative. His influence is treated in Codes 4 and 5.

Muratorian Canon: A late second-century Christian document that gives a list of the books received and not received in the churches. Explicitly included are the four Gospels. Explicitly excluded are works by

Marcion and Valentinus. This work is described in Code 5.

Nag Hammadi: Locale in the Egyptian desert where numerous Gnostic and Gnostic-like documents were found in 1945. These are known as the Nag Hammadi Library. They are discussed in Codes 1, 4, and 6.

"New" School: An increasingly influential wing of biblical scholarship claiming that the traditional history of Christianity that portrays a battle between orthodox and unorthodox camps in the second and third centuries is anachronistic and needs to be revised. This school argues that more weight needs to be given to extrabiblical materials in constructing this history. This school was discussed in Codes 4, 5, 6, and 7.

Nicea: A church council convened in A.D. 325 primarily to discuss the definition of the deity of Christ and the doctrine of God. The primary figures at Nicea were Athanasius, who argued for the full deity of Christ, and Arius, who argued that Jesus was the greatest created being. The position of Athanasius prevailed at the council. Code 5 treats what Nicea was and was not.

Opus Dei: Opus Dei is a personal Prelature of the Catholic church that helps ordinary laypeople seek holiness in everyday activities and especially through work. It was founded in 1928 by a twenty-six-year-old Catholic priest, Josemaria Escriva, who died in 1975, and was canonized by Pope John Paul II on October 6, 2002. It helps ordinary people live up to their Christian calling in their day-to-day affairs by giving them spiritual support and formation. It promotes an awareness of the universal call to holiness — the radical idea that every person is called by God to be a saint — especially holiness in and by means of one's ordinary work and daily routine. This goal is pursued through retreats, mornings/evenings of recollection, courses in philosophy and theology, personal spiritual guidance, for members first of all, but also for others who wish to avail themselves of these spiritual services. Criticism has sometimes been directed at Opus Dei because of its strong faithfulness to the pope, the bishops, and the Catholic faith. The movement is briefly noted in Code 7 and in the Introduction.

Origen: A late second-century church father. His views are noted in Codes 4 and 5.

Orthodox: A term that refers to true or accurate belief.

Pagan: A person who is not a member of

one of the monotheistic religions (Judaism, Christianity, or Islam). A pagan can worship many gods or no gods.

Pleroma: A term that means "Entirety" or "Fullness." *Pleroma* refers to the true, pure, transcendent, supreme God of the Gnostics. This idea is treated in Code 4.

Prelature: An organized group of prelates. A prelate is a serving official in the Roman Catholic Church. There are different ranks, such as father, bishop, and cardinal. Opus Dei is a prelature made up of laypeople, both men and women.

Priory of Sion: In 1956, an organization called the Priory of Sion registered with the St Julien-en-Genevois bureau of records in France. Its four officers were Andre Bonhomme, president; Jean Delaval, vice president; Pierre Plantard, secretary-general; and Armand Defago, treasurer. Whether this organization continued to exist after the resignation in 1984 of Pierre Plantard, who had become Grand Master, no one knows. The original president Andre Bonhomme made this statement on a BBC special about this mysterious group in 1996: "The Priory of Sion doesn't exist anymore. We were never involved in any activities of a political nature. It was four friends who came together to have fun. We called ourselves the

Priory of Sion because there was a mountain by the same name close by. I haven't seen Pierre Plantard in over 20 years and I don't know what he's up to but he always had a great imagination. I don't know why people try to make such a big thing out of nothing." The claim that the Priory went back to the period of the crusades is highly contested. There was an Order of Sion in this medieval period tied to an abbey, but no hard evidence that the Order ever was tied to the Knights Templar. A brief reference to this group is in Code 7.

Purist Documents: These are the alleged textual collections of the Priory, giving the "other side of the Christ story." They are part of what is an even larger alleged collection, the *Sangreal* documents or treasure.

Q: Abbreviation used in New Testament study of the Gospels for a source of Jesus' teaching that circulated in the first century. Material from this source is said to be in both Matthew and Luke and consists of slightly more than two hundred verses of those gospels. Most scholars of New Testament studies accept the idea that such a source or sources of the teaching of Jesus did circulate in the earliest period of the church. In *The Da Vinci Code* this document is a part of the large collection of secret documents. There is no manuscript of this source. Its reconstruction emerges from comparing the Gospels to each other. It is the one secret, still hidden document *The Da Vinci Code* mentions that might have existed at one time.

Rosslyn (Roslin) Chapel: A site, seven miles south of Edinburgh, Scotland, tied in legend to various documents and artifacts, including the Holy Grail. It was built in 1446 for the Prince of Orkney. This is a key site for final events in *The Da Vinci Code.*

***Sang Real* (or *Sangreal*):** A term meaning "holy blood." (See discussion of *Holy Grail.*) *The Da Vinci Code* argues that Mary Magdalene is the Holy Grail and that her sarcophagus contains these *Sangreal* documents. Among these documents are those that are alleged to reveal the bloodline of Jesus. This is discussed in Code 1.

Second Treatise of the Great Seth: This second-century Gnostic Christian work is in the form of a revelatory dialogue. It defends the idea that the Jesus who died on the cross was not the same as the Christ. So it argued for a docetic Jesus. It is treated in Code 4.

Shekinah: A term referring to the "glory of God." The idea that this term is paired

236

with the name of God, Yahweh, so that a male (Yahweh) and female (Shekinah) counterpart exists with God, is simple fabrication.

Shepherd of Hermes: An early Christian work of the mid-second century.

Sirach: A Jewish wisdom text of the second century B.C. It is noted in Code 3.

Symbology: The study of symbols.

Tatian: A student of Justin Martyr and later a follower of Valentinus. He is a second-century teacher who wrote the first harmony of Jesus' life. He is discussed in Code 5.

Tertullian: A late second- and early third-century church father. His work is noted in Codes 4 and 5.

Testimony of Truth: A short Gnostic Christian text from Nag Hammadi that is poorly preserved. A defense of Gnostic Christianity, it was likely written at the end of the second century.

Valentinus: A major teacher of Gnostic Christianity of the second century. His work comes in for focused criticism from Irenaeus and Tertullian. He is a topic of Code 4.

Yahweh: The Hebrew name for the God of Israel.